Social Adjustment
of Young Children

A Cognitive Approach
to Solving Real-Life Problems

George Spivack

Myrna B. Shure

SOCIAL
ADJUSTMENT
OF YOUNG
CHILDREN

A Cognitive Approach
to Solving Real-Life Problems

 Jossey-Bass Publishers
San Francisco • Washington • London • 1974

SOCIAL ADJUSTMENT OF YOUNG CHILDREN
A Cognitive Approach to Solving Real-Life Problems
by George Spivack and Myrna B. Shure

Copyright © 1974 by: Jossey-Bass, Inc., Publishers
615 Montgomery Street
San Francisco, California 94111

&

Jossey-Bass Limited
3 Henrietta Street
London WC2E 8LU

Library of Congress Catalogue Card Number LC 73-10942

International Standard Book Number ISBN 0-87589-207-8

Manufactured in the United States of America

JACKET DESIGN BY WILLI BAUM

FIRST EDITION

Code 7344

The Jossey-Bass
Behavioral Science Series

Special Advisors

WILLIAM E. HENRY
University of Chicago

NEVITT SANFORD
Wright Institute, Berkeley

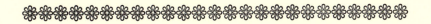

To our families:
Jane, Jonathan,
Jason, and Bob

Preface

What might an adult say to a preschool child who hits another child or grabs a toy or cries? One possible response is, "Kevin, I know you feel angry at Paul, but I can't let you hit him." Another is, "Paul doesn't like to be hit." Sean snatches a truck from Robert and the adult asks him why he has taken the truck. "I want it!" is the answer. "Wait until Robert is finished and then you can play with it," says the adult, or "Robert, you've had a long turn with the truck, and now let Sean have a turn."

In handling such behaviors as hitting and grabbing, many teachers and parents of young children demand that the behavior stop "because I said so." They often explain why the behavior is unacceptable. ("You can't hit Paul because you might hurt him.") If the hitting persists in school, the child might be isolated from the other children until he calms down or is judged to be ready to play without hitting. A more inhibited or fearful child who is standing outside the playgroup is often offered direct help by an adult. Many a teacher suggests to the group leader that "Tanya would like to play too," and "Maybe she could be the baby or help pack the suitcase."

We believe that such techniques have serious limitations if one's goal is to help children develop effective ways of handling personal and interpersonal problems. First, the adult is too often doing the thinking for the child. The child is told he should wait his turn or stay away from another child or not hit. The inhibited child standing outside the playgroup is simply put into the group. The child neither solves his problem nor is helped to discover a solution of his own. Second, the adult in attempting to help a child often assumes that the child has a real understanding of the language of emotions ("I know you feel angry") or of negation ("but I *can't* let you hit him") or of causal relationships ("because you might hurt him"). Many young children do not have mastery of the language concepts necessary to solve interpersonal problems. Even if the child uses a word, it may not have functional meaning for him in communicating and problem-solving. In the process of lengthy explanation, the adult is often not reaching the child at all. Finally, solving a problem for a child does little to help him feel good about himself. He is simply told what he can and cannot do, even though the reasons may be explained and the solution may work in that particular instance. He does not experience mastery that emerges when one has solved a problem. He may feel protected, but not competent.

Social Adjustment of Young Children describes an approach to dealing with interpersonal behavior and a carefully researched, specific intervention program. The approach is based on the conception that if individuals can be helped to develop a cognitive problem-solving style for real-life problems and to generate their own ways of solving the typical interpersonal problems that arise during their day, they will be able to cope better than before and will manifest this improvement in changes in overt behavorial adjustment. Further, to achieve this level of overt functioning developing children must first have certain language and cognitive skills needed to solve problems, and they must be taught how to use these skills in solving real interpersonal difficulties.

The kernel of this conception came into being a decade ago. One of us was having a problem in therapeutic work with a delinquent teen-ager who had gone AWOL from the residential treatment center because he wanted to purchase something in a nearby town. An attempt to explore with the youngster his awareness of the possible consequences of his act and whether he had thought of legitimate ways to get what he wanted suggested that the boy had not contemplated these issues beforehand. The youngster only repeated in therapy that he had wanted something and so went to get it. He did not seem to have an unconscious desire to get caught and be disciplined. He did not act in anger or resentment, nor was there an apparent compelling need for what he sought at the moment. The most parsimonious explanation for his behavior seemed to be that the boy just did not think and that this lack of thought had gotten him into difficulty. Further, his failure to think about implications and consequences of what he was doing could not be ascribed to a limitation in measured intellectual ability. He was a boy of above-average intelligence. Although somewhat impulsive, he was not excessively defiant or difficult to manage. When he wanted something, apparently his thinking quickly focused on consummation, with little if any focus on the details of how to get what he wanted, obstacles that might arise in getting it, the pros and cons of different courses of action, and the consequences for him and others.

This clinical incident stimulated extensive theorizing and research, especially in the Division of Research of the Department of Mental Health Sciences of Hahnemann Medical College and Hospital. What has emerged is a general, multilevel theory of healthy human functioning that has at its center the construct of interpersonal problem-solving capacity. This theory proposes that the significance of cultural, interpersonal, familial, and psychological intrapsychic events in human adjustment depends on their impact on the problem-solving capacity of the individual in his attempts to become the kind of person he wants to be. Research efforts have attempted to define and measure across a wide age-span the elements that constitute problem-solving capacity and are relevant to social adjustment. Recent effort has gone into the development of educational and treatment programs designed specifically to enhance this capacity.

As part of this effort, since 1968 we have studied the interpersonal problem-solving abilities of preschool and nine- to twelve-year-old children. We have been able to combine our clinical, theoretical, and child developmental knowledge and skills in this effort. Initial studies attempted to shed light on how well children who differ in social adjustment think through interpersonal problems and on the effect of cultural background upon this ability. These studies grappled with how to measure the quantity and quality of such interpersonal cognitive skills because no work has been done in this area. This measurement problem was enhanced when it became necessary to measure such thinking ability in four-year-old children, many of whom had modest verbal skills. It was also necessary to extricate ourselves from habits of thinking which assume that if what one studies correlates even modestly with measured intelligence, then to that extent one is not contributing anything new to an understanding of human thinking and behavior.

Our efforts since 1970 have focused largely on applying knowledge gained from these earlier studies to the development of a training program to enhance the interpersonal problem-solving thinking of young children. This process has involved us in the training of teachers and child-care personnel in a large public school system and in the measurement of thinking and behavioral adjustment of hundreds of children. It has provided information that has not only improved the program but also supplied new data and ideas about the thinking processes being trained and their underlying linguistic and conceptual elements. The training script we present in *Social Adjustment of Young Children* has been re-written numerous times to fit our improved understanding of what we are doing and to meet the practical needs of those who wish to use it. This entire process—research, program-application, and feedback—has been slow but rewarding. It has resulted in a program that has proved itself in practice and has a theoretical underpinning that allows for improvement and refinement. We can now describe this entire process and its products in sufficient detail so that others may apply the program and evaluate its effectiveness.

This book should be of interest to those studying early childhood development, those teaching young children, and those in the psychiatric and mental health fields responsible for creating and maintaining treatment programs. It should interest students of early childhood development because it focuses on interpersonal cognition. The scientific study of cognitive development has inquired in depth into mental processes and their stages, as well as into the linguistic development of young children. However, cognitive studies have largely ignored the interpersonal realm, apparently assuming that the skills needed to handle abstract, impersonal problems (such as the volume of a jar) are the same as those needed to handle interpersonal problems (such as how to get a toy from another child). Such an assumption may not be warranted.

Social Adjustment of Young Children should be of interest to teachers of young children and their aides because it focuses attention on the daily interpersonal behaviors of children, offers an understanding and approach to them, and provides a realistic and effective program script for day-care, nursery, and kindergarten settings. Staff from these settings have been intimately involved during the program development phase of our work. The material in the book should interest too those responsible for training teachers and may serve well in coursework and inservice training programs aimed generally at teaching technique and specifically at an appreciation of the teacher as a mental health agent. The training script could constitute a core curriculum for nursery schools and child-care centers.

The volume should certainly interest those working with children in the mental health field because it offers a validated treatment and primary preventive program for young children as well as an approach that is applicable in a special school, clinic, or residential treatment center. The script, which has been used by teachers and teacher aides, can be equally useful to mental health personnel in a variety of settings. It could fill a gap in the preventive mental health area for community mental health planners. Its applicability is abetted by the fact that it does not require highly specialized training or a special theoretical orientation. It is offered with the comforting knowledge that it not only makes sense but also has been shown to work in three carefully designed evaluation studies.

In presenting both the research findings and the program that has emerged from them, we have divided this book into two parts. In Part One we describe our research findings, program development, and program evaluation. Chapter One reviews our research along with the research of others interested in bridging the gap between problem-solving and human adjustment. Chapter Two describes how the theory and research findings were translated into a cognitive training program and presents the principles underlying the approach taken in designing the script. Chapter Three is an outline of the formal training script for both preschool and kindergarten children. Our purpose is to provide the reader with an understanding of the script elements and what they are designed to achieve by way of cognitive change. Chapter Four gives some hints to those who wish to use the script with children exhibiting certain "difficult" behaviors, and Chapters Five and Six provide specific examples of and general guidelines on how to employ the basic training approach with children informally throughout the day.

Chapters Seven and Eight describe results of studies and interviews designed to evaluate the effectiveness of the program on the cognitive efficiency and behavioral adjustment of preschool children. Data from three carefully designed studies are presented in Chapter Seven, and Chapter Eight offers observations of teachers and parents on the behavior of the children involved in the program.

In Chapter Nine we share with the reader our experience in getting the program operative in Philadelphia Get Set classrooms over a four-year period. We hope that our advice on how to train teachers, consult with them, and work with school administrators will be of practical use to those who wish to use the program in their own settings. In Chapter Ten we spell out the implications of our approach for both clinical practice and research, and suggest directions for future study.

In Part Two, Chapter Eleven presents the detailed working script to be used in carrying out the program. It provides general instructions, describes the specific day-by-day games and dialogues, and lists the materials needed. Chapter Twelve describes in detail the cognitive and behavioral adjustment measures we have developed to evaluate the program in a variety of settings.

The development of this program has brought us into contact with many schools, teachers, clinicians, and parents, without whom the research and program development would have been impossible.

Milton Goldberg, executive director of early childhood programs of the school district of Philadelphia, has supported the program from its inception, as have the administrative staff of the Philadelphia Get Set day-care program: Jeffrey O. Jones (director), Rosemary Mazzatenta (assistant director), and Vivian Ray (chief psychologist.) Many teachers and day-care personnel have participated both in developing the script and in experimenting with it. Special appreciation goes to Richard Benowitz, Mary S. Cochran, Jean Fargo, E. Delores Flint, Lorretta E. Howard, Alice Jones, Molly McLaughlin, Mary Seiss, Sally Silver, Pamela Wallace, and Sandra B. Williams. Without the support of Lafayette Powell, currently assistant director of special education, the numerous problems in instituting new research and training programs in a large educational setting would not have been solved.

For the interdisciplinary enterprise from research to training program, little could have been accomplished without the flexible and creative efforts of Marsha Bloom, Rochelle Newman, and Stanley Silver, our research assistants. They performed a wide variety of tasks from data collection and analysis to substitute teaching and offered invaluable suggestions throughout the development of the program. For the mental health program developed and evaluated in a school and preschool setting yet sponsored by a department of a medical college, Van Buren O. Hammett, then chairman of the Department of Mental Health Sciences, and Clifford J. Bodarky, deputy chairman and director of the Hahnemann Community Mental Health Center, deserve recognition. Both supported the development of this program by affording us the opportunity to research new areas and develop innovative mental health programs that would benefit an inner-city community. During a period when pressures for immediate research results were mounting, these unique mental health administrators were also willing to support studies with a potential for broad and long-term returns. We hope the results have justified the farsighted position they have taken regarding mental health research.

Initial research work was supported by the Hahnemann NIH institutional grant 720-20-0150 through its daughter grant mechanism. The last two years of development were supported in part by grant R01-MH20372, awarded by the Applied Research

Branch of the National Institute of Mental Health, Washington, D.C. Yet even with these funds and the cooperation of other agencies and schools, the entire story would be incomplete without recognizing the secretarial assistance of Joanne Street, Bertha Washington, and Patricia Patterson. With patience and good humor, they have tolerated our scribbles, altered manuscripts, last-minute changes, and unexpected deadlines. We also wish to acknowledge the research assistance of Paul Barr, Samuel Mosca, Lorraine Bittner, and Dorothy Heard, Psychological Services, Philadelphia Get Set, day-care program, and the statistical consultation of Leona Aiken, Temple University, and Kurt Ebert, University of Pennsylvania.

Philadelphia   GEORGE SPIVACK
September 1973   MYRNA B. SHURE

Contents

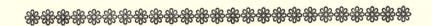

Social Adjustment
of Young Children

A Cognitive Approach
to Solving Real-Life Problems

I

Problem-Solving and Mental Health

The mental health approach described in this book focuses on the ability to think through ways to solve real-life problems. When a person is confronted with an unmet need or a conflict, he must be able to recognize the problem and see ways of solving it. Such problem-solving may involve understanding the nature of the problem and careful step-by-step planning of ways to reach a goal. Sifting through alternative possibilities and weighing their possible consequences relative to action are also aspects of solving real-life problems.

Suppose that a man moves into a new neighborhood and wants to make new friends. If he concentrates only on the goal, such as making friends, without thinking of the various means to obtain it and their potential consequences, he may in fact alienate the very people he wants to like him. But if he plans ways to attract

1

those people and can turn to alternative ways if his early ideas prove ineffective, he will increase his chances of success and relieve his loneliness. An individual who is preoccupied with a goal to the exclusion of thoughts about means to obtain it may make impulsive mistakes. He may then become frustrated and aggressive or try to escape from the problem entirely by withdrawing or deceiving himself about his personal involvement in it. In either case his initial needs remains unsatisfied. If such failures occur repeatedly, maladaptive behaviors are bound to ensue.

Although it may seem self-evident that such thought processes are important in human adjustment, the fact remains that such processes have rarely been studied experimentally, and there have few attempts to intervene directly in these processes as a way of affecting behavioral adjustment. Clinicians and educators have always assumed that if an individual could be relieved of interfering emotional discomfort he would be free to think clearly and see his way through everyday problem situations without further guidance. The opposite idea, that being able to think through and solve real-life problems might reduce emotional discomfort or behavioral maladjustment, has not been the focus of treatment or educational programs. This primacy of problem-solving is part of a general theory of the relationship between problem-solving ability and mental health proposed by Spivack (1973).

Our approach asserts that interpersonal problem-solving is too crucial to remain unexamined. Although some writers such as Jahoda (1953, 1958) have suggested that the capacity to solve problems in real-life situations is one criterion for defining positive mental health, most research in problem-solving ability is concerned not with interpersonal real-life situations but with the impersonal world. The study of human problem-solving has a long and respected history in psychology and has been reviewed periodically (Duncan, 1959; Davis, 1966). The focus of these studies, however, has been solely on the measurement of cognitive styles and abilities when the person is confronted with impersonal tasks. In these studies the person may be confronted with a puzzle or an anagram problem or asked to decide which color light will flash next on a screen, based on his experience with previous color sequences shown. Other tasks are essentially tests of general reasoning ability or concept formation: the individual has to solve syllogisms or discover how items on a table are the same or why they go together. Tasks requiring intellectual creativity have also at times been used to exemplify the ability to solve problems. It has been pointed out that the approach taken in measuring such ability has reflected the theoretical disposition of the investigators (see Coates, Alluisi, and Morgan, 1971). The gestalt approach has emphasized the insightful nature of problem-solving (see Asher, 1963; Sheerer, 1963) whereas others treat the issue in terms of information-processing (see Posner, 1965). Still others touch on the issue out of their general interest in the makeup of intellectual ability (see Merrifield, Guilford, Christensen, and Frick, 1962).

Other studies of impersonal problem-solving skills have attempted to determine developmental differences from age group to age group, and differences between the advantaged and disadvantaged, or to learn more about thinking processes per se (see Gray and Miller, 1967).

To date no one has suggested that it may be necessary to distinguish between the problem-solving processes called forth by such impersonal intellectual tasks and the thinking demanded when one is confronted with interpersonal problems. Simon and Newell (1971) make no reference to interpersonal functioning in their review of cognitive problem-solving. There is no evidence that the ability to solve a paper-and-pencil maze test indicates how well a person will handle a conflict with a friend. Solving impersonal problems does not allow one to become personally involved except to the extent that he is ego-involved in the task. The substance of the task is unrelated to the individual as a person. The problem is not designed to tap one's personal or interpersonal hopes and aspirations. It has no intimate relationship to him.

Our approach is quite different. It focuses on problem-solving skills that indicate how a person views and handles personal needs or interpersonal situations which require resolution. Rather than having to solve an abstract puzzle a person might have to solve the problem of getting something he wants from someone else, or of dealing with an interpersonal difficulty. A child might have to discover what to do if he wants a toy and someone else has it or what he might do to keep his mother from being angry because he broke her flowerpot. How he thinks in such circumstances is relevant to his ability to handle everyday life problems—whether and how he thinks about the interpersonal situation, considers different things he might do and their implications for him as well as others, and sees outcomes relative to his own desires and feelings.

Some recent studies have focused attention on the relationship between problem-solving and human adjustment, although they are few in number. Meichenbaum and Goodman (1971), for example, have conducted studies based on the assumption that children act impulsively because they do not think through the problem confronting them. However, the problem presented to the children was impersonal. Meichenbaum and Goodman found it possible to train second-grade children first to talk out loud and then to themselves about a problem. The children could be trained to instruct themselves while carrying out a variety of paper-and-pencil tasks varying in difficulty. As a consequence, impulsive handling of other paper-and-pencil tasks was reduced. There was no significant change in impulsive behavior in the classroom, however. Levinson and Neuringer (1971) propose that suicidal behavior among adolescents may reflect diminished problem-solving ability. They demonstrated that a group of suicidal adolescents were less able than were other abnormal and normal adolescents to shift to an efficient method of drawing routes on a paper-and-pencil map task. No explanation is offered as to why normal and nonsuicidal adolescents in their study did not differ on this measure of flexibility of thinking.

Moving from the realm of impersonal problem-solving, a few studies have dealt with thinking skills in the area of personal and interpersonal events. Muuss (1960a) and Ojemann (1967) report on the causal thinking of children six to twelve years of age. Their social causality test presents typical interpersonal problem situations in paragraph form, and the child is asked to read each and select the solution that he feels explains the situation. The choices made are scored as reflecting the youngster's appreciation of cause-and-effect dynamics in human relations. Their studies indicate that teachers may, by using certain prepared materials and techniques, enhance such causal thinking. The relationship of causal thinking to adjustment, however, is measured by asking the child to answer questions on paper. His answers are taken to indicate the degree of his adjustment along certain personality dimensions as well as his general level of mental health. Unfortunately none of these studies measures behavioral adjustment as observed in the classroom or elsewhere. According to Muuss (1960b, p. 155), "a child might operate causally in his thinking processes and thus be able to give the kind of answer that is considered as indicative of mental health while still unable to emotionally apply causal thinking to actual situations such as conflict. . . . Thus, there is a great need for an investigation of the same variables according to more direct behavior indices of mental health."

Despite this limitation these studies of causal thinking are important in suggesting two directions for study. First they suggest that solving human problems may make a significant contribution to behavioral adjustment and that such thinking may be altered by direct intervention in the classroom. Second their data suggest that causal thinking about social events is not the same as causal thinking about impersonal events. Muuss (1960a) reports that although social causality test scores do not relate to measured intelligence, scores on their causality test describing impersonal events do. This finding is consistent with that of Platt, Spivack, and Bloom (1971), who have consistently found low correlations between interpersonal cognitive problem-solving skills and measures of general intellectual originality of thinking. Beyond establishing some minimal requirement of intellectual aptitude in general, there is no reason to assume that competence in solving impersonal, abstract tasks would contribute significantly to problem-solving in real-life interpersonal affairs.

A model of interpersonal problem-solving thinking in relation to psychological competence has been presented by D'Zurrilla and Goldfried (1971). They describe what they view as likely stages of problem-solving, present research evidence that they feel is consistent with the notion of such stages, and suggest how training and therapy may be viewed as teaching the person how to solve problems. Unfortunately the problem-solving research they quote deals almost exclusively with impersonal tasks. Whether research can validate their suggestions for training and treatment about interpersonal problems will have to await further evidence.

Teaching a person how to solve a specific problem has been shown to be somewhat effective in changing behavior. Giebink, Stover, and Fahl (1968) taught a small number of ten- to-twelve year-old impulsive boys alternative adaptive ways to handle frustrating situations. They found that boys who received instructions in what to do improved in their ability to handle frustrating situations more than did boys who did not receive instruction. However, as they recognize (1968, p. 368), "it is possible that generalization might have been greater if the study had been carried on over a greater length of time [two weeks]," and "it seems likely that the responses that were taught were relatively specific to the situations and were so regarded by [the boys]."

Another training program was conducted by Holzworth (1964). He taught socially acceptable verbal solutions and consequences of problem situations to four-year olds displaying deviant behavior in the classroom. However, he found significant improvement in only one behavioral dimension, that of isolated play. Since both Giebink and others, and Holzworth studied only six children, only two of whom were trained in the latter study, it is difficult to assess the significance of their results.

The training program presented in this book was designed with the goal of teaching personal and interpersonal problem-solving skills that children could incorporate and use when confronted with a variety of typical problem situations. First we and our colleagues conducted a number of background studies to identify the kinds of thinking skills lacking in poorly adjusted individuals. The first studies reported dealt with adolescents, preadolescents, and adults. The studies of four-year olds tapped three facets of the ability to solve real-life problems and the relationship of these facets to behavioral adjustment in a variety of classroom situations. Finally studies were done to train these thinking skills and to assess improvement in behavioral adjustment.

The first study relating interpersonal problem-solving skills to behavioral adjustment was conducted by Spivack and Levine (1963). The subjects consisted of residentially placed, emotionally disturbed, adolescent boys characterized as impulsive. This group of teenagers was administered three tasks of particular relevance to the present issues as part of a broad battery of tests and measures.

The first task was step-by-step planning. Each youngster was tested for his ability to plan careful step-by-step means to reach a stated goal, a process called *means-ends thinking*. Such planning includes insight and forethought to forestall or circumvent obstacles that might hinder a particular plan, as well as having at one's command alternative routes if such an obstacle is realistically or psychologically insurmountable. Another aspect of such planning is an awareness that goals are not always reached immediately and that certain times are more advantageous for action than others.

The means-ends problem-solving test consisted of a group of stories, each simulating a real-life problem to be solved. The youngster was given the beginning and end of each story and was asked to "fill in the middle," "tell what happens in between," or "tell how the ending got to be that way." He was encouraged to make up a story plot but was otherwise allowed to approach the problem in any way he wished. One such plot is given here: "One day George was standing around with some other kids when one of the kids said something real nasty to George. George got very mad. He got so mad he decided to get even with the other boy. The story ends with George happy because he got even. What happens in between one of the kids saying something real nasty to George and when he is very happy because he got even?" Other story motives included sexual attraction, needing money, wanting revenge, and wanting friends.

Spivack and Levine found that impulsive adolescents exhibited less ability than their normal peers to conceptualize means in achieving the satisfactions or goals presented. When motivated in fantasy, their thinking moved to consummation with insufficient consideration of how to get there and inadequate awareness of obstacles that might have to be overcome. Such means-ends thinking was not found to be related to measured intelligence.

The second task was consequential thinking. Each youngster was presented with stories in which the teen-age protagonist was confronted with a typical adolescent temptation. In one instance he was tempted to socialize rather than study. The youngster was asked to complete the story, indicating what goes on in the tempted protagonist's mind before he decides to do something and what happens after that. Here is a sample story: "Bill loves to go hunting but is not allowed to go hunting by himself. One weekend his parents go on a trip and he remains at home by himself. He has a new shotgun he received recently and a box of shells. He looks out the window at the nearby woods and is tempted to go out hunting. Tell everything that goes on in Bill's mind and then what happens." The results indicated that the impulsive teen-agers were less prone than their normal peers to consider the pros and cons of possible actions before deciding what might be done. They were also less prone to conceptualize consequences of their fantasied acts, whether the latter indicated giving in to temptation or not.

The third task was planning and foresight. This procedure involved a simple questionnaire on which each youngster recorded instances when he planned or exhibited foresight. On a six-point scale from always to never, one question was "Do you leave vacation plans to the last minute?" Again the impulsive group obtained scores that reflected less planning and foresight than the normal group, consistent with their other behaviors.

The conclusion drawn from all these results was that impulsive adolescents suffer from a cognitive problem-solving deficiency which gets them into difficulties with others and brings on failure when they are confronted with important life situations. The implications of these results for the education of such youngsters were subsequently explored by Spivack (1966), who spelled out educational procedures predicated on these deficiencies.

Further work was done by Platt, Altman, and Altman (1973) with adolescents admitted to psychiatric hospitals. They examined sensitivity to the existence of life problems, ability to think of alternative solutions to such problems, readiness to view consequences of acts, social cause-and-effect thinking, and means-ends thinking.

Sensitivity to problems was assessed by directly asking the youngster: "What kinds of problems do you think people have in life?" A standardized probing technique was developed, and responses were scored in terms of the number of distinct problem areas the youngster could conceptualize. To measure capacity to conceptualize alternative solutions to a problem, the youngster was told: "Now I am going to tell you some things that happen to a to a person, and I want you to think of all the things he could do about it." Again a standardized set of probing questions was employed to help elicit differing solutions to each problem. An example of a problem follows: "John wants to watch his favorite TV program but his friend is watching another program. What can John do so he can have a turn watching TV?"

Readiness to view the consequences of acts and means-ends thinking were assessed using a story-telling procedure similar to that of Spivack and Levine (1963). Social cause-and-effect thinking was measured using a method the wording of which was adapted from Biber and Lewis (1949). Four interpersonal situations were described (for example, "Jim felt very mad and he's walking home with his friend. What is he saying to his friend?"). Again, with probing questions, responses were elicited that could be analyzed relative to whether or not there was a focus on the cause of the situation presented.

When compared with a normal control group, the hospitalized adolescents were less able to conceptualize alternative solutions to problems and reported fewer useful means to achieve an already defined goal. The groups did not differ in social causal thinking, consequential thinking, or sensitivity to problems.

Platt and Spivack (1972a) examined problem-solving ability in adult psychiatric patients and reported that such patients exhibit fewer problem-solving means than normals (employing the same means-ends measure). The patient means when produced were often found to be irrelevant to the life problem faced. Platt and Spivack (1973a) also reported that the content of problem-solving means among patients is different than that of normals. Normals were found to conceptualize the idea of thinking or planning whereas patients were prone only to conceptualize action that may be taken.

The intimate relation between problem-solving ability and behavioral adjustment was confirmed in a third study (Platt and Spivack, 1972b), which demonstrated that in a group of adult patients the quality of problem-solving cognition was significantly related to degree of social competence before hospitalization. The measure of social competence has been related positively to good treatment prognosis and other measures of psychological health. Means-ends thinking ability has also been shown to differ among groups of normal individuals who differ in overall life competence

(Platt, Spivack, and Bloom, 1971) despite the absence of a relationship between such thinking and measures of IQ, scholastic test scores, and originality of thinking.

Platt and Spivack (1973b) have reported on performance among adult psychiatric patients employing all the tasks used by Platt, Altman, and Altman. The results duplicate those with adolescents, suggesting among both adolescents and adults a relationship between psychiatric status and ability to generate alternative solutions, and ability to generate means-ends thinking. The finding of a relationship between means-ends thinking and degree of maladjustment in both normal and psychiatric groups reinforces the specific relevance of such thinking processes to human adjustment. Unlike the findings with adolescents, among adults normals were significantly more prone than patients to think in terms of social causality and consequences.

Shure and Spivack (1972b) have studied means-ends thinking among ten- to twelve-year-old disturbed and normal youngsters as well as youngsters of this age differing in social class. The same format for the means-ends measure was employed as in the studies of adolescents and adults except that the content of the stories was changed to tap interpersonal problems appropriate to this age group. The behaviorally disturbed youngsters in both middle and lower social class groups were found to exhibit fewer means-ends thoughts than normal youngsters, and their problem-solving thoughts were more limited to pragmatic, impulsive, and aggressive means.

An example of the distinct differences in step-by-step means-ends thinking is illustrated here, using the story of the child who got even when another child made a nasty remark.

Disturbed child's story: "He hit him, talked to him, kicked him, told him, scratched him. Throw a stone. Pick up something and throw it at him. Push him in the mud. Hit his back against the wall. Hit him on the head. Push him in the water. Then he got even."

Normal child's story: "She would have a party that Saturday night to get revenge. A few days before the party, Amy went down to the drugstore that specialized in fake pranks. She found a package which held three fake ice-cubes with a fly in the middle of it which made it look realistic. . . . Each person was to get a glass of Coke. In one of the glasses she dropped the fake ice-cubes instead of the real ones. She saved the glass specifically for the kid who she planned to get revenge."

Shure and Spivack (1970a) studied the relationship between behavioral adjustment and ability to imagine alternative solutions to problems among normal fifth-graders from lower- and middle-class settings. In this procedure the youngster was presented with interpersonal problem situations, such as "Johnny wants his friend to go to the playground with him after school, but his friend doesn't want to go. What can Johnny do to get his friend to go with him?" After responding the youngster was asked "What else can he do?" until he said he could think of nothing else. The behavioral adjustment of each youngster was assessed by his teacher using a well-standardized rating scale for overt classroom behavior. The results indicated that youngsters rated as able to adapt in the classroom were able to imagine a variety of interpersonal problem solutions on the cognitive task. This was true irrespective of social class and measured intelligence.

Larcen, Spivack, and Shure (1972) adapted the means-ends procedure for nine- through twelve-year olds and related performance to behavioral adjustment within a group of residentially placed, dependent-neglected children. Consequential and social causal thinking were also measured. Results indicated that even in this homogeneous group of special children, the degree of behavioral adjustment in the residential environment was significantly related to the amount of appropriate means-ends thinking and social causal thinking, although not consequential thinking. Again measured IQ did not significantly correlate with any of the other measures.

Shure and Spivack (1970b) and Shure, Spivack, and Jaeger (1971) examined how specific aspects of problem-solving ability relate to behavioral adjustment among four- to five-year-old nursery school children. The procedures were modified and supplemented with pictures to meet the abilities and excite the interest of children this age. Pilot studies indicated that the story-telling means-ends procedure was too demanding for this age group. Because these studies form the background of the training program to be described, the testing procedures that constituted the evaluation of the program's effectiveness are discussed in more detail here. (For specifics of testing, see Chapter Twelve.)

The investigators developed a unique measure to assess the number and variety of alternative solutions given by the children to typical, age-relevant problem situations.

The Preschool Interpersonal Problem-Solving (PIPS) Test was created to tap each child's ability to name alternative solutions to two life-related types of problems: ways a child might obtain a toy from another child and ways a child might avert his mother's anger caused by his damaging property.

For all peer problems the child had to conceptualize ways one child might obtain a toy from another. The experimenter showed the subject three pictures, two of children and one of a toy, and then (for instance) said: "Here's Johnny (*pointing to picture*) and here's Jim (*pointing to other picture*). Johnny is playing with this shovel (*pointing to picture of shovel*), and he has been playing with it for a long time. Now Jim wants a chance to play with this shovel. What can Jim do or say so he can have a chance to play with this shovel?"

The procedure was designed to elicit as many different solutions as possible from each child as he went through variations of the problem situation. New characters and a new toy were presented to elicit a new response and to maintain interest. The instructions were worded to encourage the child to give a different solution to each new toy and set of characters. The child was presented with a minimum of seven similar peer-toy situations, but if seven different solutions were given the experimenter continued until the child ran out of options.

For authority problems the child had to conceptualize specific ways to avert his mother's anger for acts of property damage, such as breaking her favorite flowerpot. The same procedure was followed: after one solution, new characters and a new act of property damage were presented and a different solution was sought.

The major behavioral indexes of adjustment were the child's rated impatience, his display of emotional control, and the amount of physical or verbal aggression shown in the classroom.

In the first study in the series Shure and Spivack (1970b)

discovered a relationship between number of different options presented in peer and authority problem situations on the one hand and both school behavioral adjustment and socioeconomic level on the other. Children from poverty areas (in contrast to middle-class children), as well as the poorly adjusted children in both social class groups, provided a narrower range of solutions to the problems presented. Lower-class children also gave solutions that were more aggressive (for example, to get a toy: "grab it" or "hit him" in contrast to "ask him," "I'll let you have my doll," "let's play together," or some other nonforceful response). In addition lower-class children and the poorly adjusted children in both social class groups gave more irrelevant solutions.

The data enrich and are consistent with a variety of findings demonstrating social class differences in cognitive functioning. The new dimension added by these findings suggests that children from the lower class are relatively deficient in conceptualizing relevant solutions to fairly typical social problems confronting them daily and that this relative deficiency bears on their behavioral adjustment in the classroom. These data suggest also that children may behave differently not only because they conceive of different types of solutions but also because they do not think of the variety of alternative solutions which could be used in the situation and which if considered might help them avoid difficulties and frustration. If effective problem-solving depends on exploration of available options, lower-class children as well as poorly adjusted children are less equipped to think effectively and thus solve problems.

In the second study Shure, Spivack, and Jaeger (1971) added measures of consequential thinking and causal thinking to their battery of tests to gain a comprehensive picture of problem-solving ability in four-year olds and to assess which of these cognitive skills relate to behavioral adjustment in the classroom. Attention in this study focused on the cognitive problem-solving skills of children from poor families who at a very early age had shown deficiencies relative to their middle-class agemates.

The measure of alternative thinking remained the same as in the first study of four-year olds. The measures of consequential thinking and causality used with older children were simplified for use with very young children. The measure of consequential thinking was similar to the PIPS test except that the child was given a solution to the problem and asked to tell what might happen next. Using the peer situation from the PIPS test the examiner showed the child the three pictures and repeated the original problem with a solution: "Johnny had this truck and he was playing with it. Jim wanted to play with this truck. So Jim grabbed—you know, snatched that truck. What might happen next in the story?" If the child did not respond the examiner said: "Tell me, what does Johnny do after Jim snatches the truck?" After one response the child was shown a new set of pictures and was asked for a different ending. He was given a minimum of five sets of pictures, each set depicting the hypothetical child as having grabbed the toy from another child. The examiner tried to elicit a new ending from the child for each set. The procedure was repeated with a second solution to the same problem, that of wanting a toy, in which the child was told: "Bobby asked Tom for the drum. He said, 'Can I play with it?' What might happen next in the story?" If no response was offered, the examiner said, "Tell me, what does Tom do after Bob asks him for it?"

The test for causal thinking measured the child's general inclination to think of cause and effect when presented with a hypothetical event. Adapted from Biber and Lewis (1949), the causality test requires the child to tell what a hypothetical child would say to his mother (or his friend) about the event described. For example: "Billy's knee is bleeding. He is talking to his mother. What do you think he is saying to her?" Such responses as "I fell down" or "someone hit me" were judged to be causal because they reveal sensitivity to what events may have caused the situation. For credit to be given, the response had to indicate a possible cause *of* the event, not what might be caused *by* the event. Therefore a response like "I need a Band-Aid because my knee is bleeding" was not viewed as causal. Another type of statement described people's feelings. For example: "Bob is real mad. After a while he sees his friend. What do you think he is saying to him?" A causal response was "I got spanked for nothin'." A noncausal one might be "I want to go home" or "Let's go play."

The youngsters were divided into three behavioral adjustment groups according to ratings made by the children's teachers and classroom aides. The two aberrant-behavior groups consisted of those judged to be impulsive (children whose behavioral ratings exceeded those of the "average child" on the factors tapping impatience, overemotionality, and excessive aggression) and those judged to be inhibited (children whose adjustment ratings were so far below those of the "average child" that they were considered maladaptively shy, fearful, or withdrawn). The adjusted group were those rated as like the "average child" and in other respects not within the maladaptive ranges. (See Chapter Eleven for details of measurement devices.)

The results of this study showed that among 62 four-year-old Get Set (Head Start) children, cognitive problem-solving skills were distinctly superior among those judged as adjusted in their classroom behavior. The four-year olds who could conceptualize the greatest number of different and relevant solutions to real-life problems (as measured by the PIPS test) were those who were able to wait their turn and not nag when they could not have what they wanted, those who were not likely to show overemotionality when things did not go their way, and those who were not likely to show exsive verbal or physical aggression toward their peers. Those judged as impulsive and those judged as inhibited showed about the same levels of deficiency, indicating that youngsters maladaptive at either behavioral extreme were not able to think through ways to solve typical problems successfully. Scores on the *Peabody Picture Vocabulary Test,* measures of ability to use the English language, and sex of child did not significantly affect the results.

There was also evidence of contrasting content of thought in the superior and inferior problem-solvers. Inferior cognitive problem-solvers were more likely than superior problem-solvers to give forceful solutions such as "grab it" or "hit him." There was also a trend suggesting that of those who conceptualized only two categories, one of which was forceful and one nonforceful, inferior problem-solvers were more likely than superior problem-solvers to express the forceful solution first.

The results for consequential and causal thinking were less impressive. Although both related to ability to conceptualize solutions, they did not relate to behavioral adjustment. Poorly adjusted youngsters were able to conceptualize consequences to an act as well as the adjusted and were also as inclined to give a causal statement when given the opportunity.

In a study the following year, Shure and Spivack (1972a) redesigned the measure of consequential thinking. The grabbing-from-a-peer situation was retained. The second situation was changed so that each hypothetical child performed the same act, such as having taken a neighbor's dog without permission. The causal situations were changed, and little wooden dolls to represent the characters were added to maintain interest. A total of 100 four-year-old Get Set children were given all three tests. The findings were the same as in the previous study: ability to conceptualize alternative solutions to real-life problems was markedly superior among well-adjusted youngsters, but consequential and causal thinking did not relate to behavioral adjustment.

A final study by Shure, Newman, and Silver (1973) involved 257 Get Set children. Considering its size, the detailed statistical analyses performed, and the significance of the results for this book, this study is discussed in some detail here.

Each child was again administered the PIPS test and the revised measure of social causality. Because of the importance of IQ the Stanford-Binet was administered to each child. The children were again classified into impulsive, overly inhibited, and behaviorally adjusted groups on the basis of teacher ratings.

The measure of consequential thinking was again modified to improve its sensitivity to individual differences. The peer social situation remained unchanged. The child-adult situation was now changed so that each new presentation of characters depicted the child taking a different object from an adult without first asking. For example, the first child was depicted as having taken a neighbor's dog for a walk without asking. The second showed him as having taken a flashlight. The basic situation, that of having taken something without asking, remained the same. The idea was to determine how many different consequences the child could give to the same act. To maintain interest, the objects taken were changed after each consequence was offered. A second change was instituted. In the earlier studies the pictures used for the consequences test were the same as those used in the PIPS test. It was decided to dissociate the two tests by using wooden stick figures for testing consequences.

Again these changes were made to improve sensitivity of measurement.

New measures were added in this extensive study. The children were rated on a number of scales that defined the quality of each child's adjustment in nursery school. Each child was also tested to assess his appreciation of the words *and* and *not*. The purpose was to determine the validity of the assumption that before a child can think of alternative solutions he must appreciate the linguistic concepts implied by these terms. Thinking in terms of options implies that the person is able to conceptualize doing one thing *and* another or is able to think he will do this and *not* that. In measuring understanding of the concept *and*, the tester asked a question that required the child to report a number of examples. The measure was whether or not the child used the word *and* in his enumerating. In measuring understanding of the word *not*, the tester gave instructions for a task and then asked the child a question. To answer the question properly the child had to understand the word *not* because it was a significant element of the instructions. For example the child was shown a picture of a box and a pencil, and the investigator said: "I am thinking of the pencil. I am *not* thinking of the————."

The relationships found between the three problem-solving abilities (alternatives, consequences, and causality) and behavioral adjustment confirmed some earlier findings and expanded others.

Findings replicating earlier studies indicate that youngsters most able to conceptualize relevant alternative solutions to typical problems were least likely to exhibit impatient and nagging behaviors, overemotionality, and aggressive and dominating behaviors. Again there were no sex differences in findings, and differential ability to conceptualize alternative solutions was found not to be a function of IQ or mere verbalization while being tested. Data also replicated earlier work indicating that better problem-solvers, in comparison with less able peers, are more likely to produce relevant solutions first in their thinking and are better able to conceptualize solutions that go beyond the use of direct force.

Data going beyond those of previous work indicate that although impulsive youngsters are less able to conceptualize alternatives than their adjusted peers, inhibited youngsters are even more deficient in this respect. Further, the ability to conceptualize alternative consequences relates significantly to behavioral adjustment independent of the findings regarding alternative thinking. A stepwise discriminant analysis revealed that although a child's PIPS score significantly predicted whether or not he would be classified as behaviorally adjusted, knowledge of his ability to conceptualize consequences added the necessary ingredient to predict whether (if maladjusted) he would fall into the impulsive or inhibited subgroup. Moreover the markedly deficient cognitive performance of the inhibited children was not a function of inability or unwillingness to talk while being tested. The number of verbal statements they made, including irrelevancies and repetitions of earlier responses, was of the same magnitude as that of the other behavioral groups on all cognitive problem-solving tests.

While causal thinking correlated with behavioral adjustment, knowledge of causal thinking did not improve ability to predict level of adjustment once knowledge of the other thinking skills and IQ were known. It seems surprising that consequential thinking relates to adjustment more clearly than causal thinking. Both seem to entail relating one event to another in time. If a child can think of a consequence of an act, it would seem reasonable to expect that the child would be quick to see a cause (for example, "he hit me back *because* I hit him first"). Whether causal thinking is important for problem-solving in four-year olds cannot be ascertained until further revisions of the measuring procedures have been tested.

The analyses of the linguistic (*and* and *not*) scores added important information about the processes involved in problem-solving. The appreciation of the meaning of these words was significantly related both to alternative thinking (as predicted) and overt behavioral adjustment. This finding raised the possibility that adjustment depended directly on linguistic knowledge and not on intermediate problem-solving as hypothesized. Discriminant analyses clarified this issue by demonstrating that scores on the linguistic measure added no power to the PIPS test in predicting behavioral adjustment, whereas the cognitive measure did add significantly to the linguistic measure in the prediction of behavioral adjustment. In support of the assumption underlying the study, these data indicate that certain linguistic skills are basic to both problem-solving and thinking, which in turn is a critical determinant of behavioral adjustment. This is not to say that the words *and* and *not* are the only prerequisite language concepts necessary for problem-solving but that a thorough understanding of problem-solving must include knowledge of certain linguistic concepts.

Considering the importance of IQ, analyses were run to assess the extent to which measured intelligence influences the relationship between cognitive and behavioral adjustment measures. The correlations between IQ and ability to think in terms of alternatives, consequences, and causality were all low but statistically significant (0.38, 0.27, and 0.34 respectively). A number of discriminant analyses were then done to assess the significance of general intellectual ability for the issues at stake. These analyses indicate that knowledge of IQ adds nothing to the power of the cognitive measures in predicting behavioral adjustment. Reversing these analyses, it was discovered that knowledge of alternative thinking ability adds significantly to IQ in predicting adjustment. These data indicate that the relevance of IQ to behavioral adjustment is accounted for in the measure of alternative thinking. The extent to which intelligence affects level of adjustment seems to be determined by the extent to which the IQ measures interpersonal problem-solving thinking.

Analyses of the other scales defining the quality of classroom adjustment added further insights into the significance of problem-solving thinking for adjustment. These scales measured each child's attentiveness, tendency to make irrelevant remarks, initiative in the group, degree of participation in group discussion, concern for others, extent of being liked by peers, ability to work autonomously, and comprehension of what goes on in the classroom. Both the ability to think of alternative solutions and the appreciation of consequences relate to these measures, even after partialing out the effect of measured IQ. The strongest relationships with the cognitive measures emerge with the scales measuring initiative, concern for others, being liked by peers, and autonomy of functioning. Stepwise regression analyses were performed to get a closer view of the nature of these relationships. In both the measures of initiative and autonomy of functioning in the classroom, the ability to think in terms of alternatives as well as IQ accounts for a significant proportion of variance. The two most interpersonal measures (concern for others and being liked by peers) are completely unaffected by IQ once the ability to conceptualize alternative solutions has been accounted for. When considering concern for others, the linguistic measure and alternative thinking were the issues. When considering being liked by peers, alternative thinking ability was the explanation. These findings confirm the initial hypothesis of the project, which proposed that certain forms of cognitive problem-solving have specific relevance to how well individuals solve personal and interpersonal problems, that these cognitive processes are not merely (if at all) what is measured by IQ tests or other measures of impersonal problem-solving, and that both degree and quality of behavioral adjustment are better understood when we appreciate interpersonal problem-solving cognition.

In summary the data clearly indicate that these investigations have uncovered an area of thought process which bears a direct relationship to human adjustment. These processes involve sensitivity to human problems, ability to imagine alternative courses of action, ability to conceptualize means to solve a problem, and sensitivity to consequences and cause and effects in human behavior. These human problem-solving skills have relevance to human adjustment across a wide age span, a broad range of human adaptive ability, and for all socioeconomic groups. There is no reason to believe that these processes constitute a single ability; rather they comprise a grouping of abilities that are related to each other. There is also reason to believe that these thinking skills differ in their significance for human adjustment depending on the age of the person. It is clear that two key abilities across all ages are the ability to imagine alternative solutions to problems and the ability to conceptualize means and potential obstacles in moving toward a goal. These cognitive problem-solving skills are not merely one component of intelligence or at least what intelligence tests measure. Evidence to date also indicates that these cognitive abilities are not the same as the abilities tapped when one has to solve purely impersonal, intellectual tasks.

The results specific to four-year olds indicate that behavioral adjustment relates significantly to ability to conceptualize alternative solutions and to a lesser extent sensitivity to consequences. The results of these research studies define the goals and significance of the training program to be described. The hypothesis is that one should be able to enhance the personal adjustment of young children if one can enhance their ability to see a human problem, their appreciation of different ways of handling it, and their sensitivity to the potential consequences of what they do.

2

From Theory to Training Program

The background research provided us with a springboard from which to test our hypothesis that certain cognitive problem-solving skills are a prerequisite condition for behavioral adjustment. If it could be shown that intervention which enhances these thinking skills also improves adjustment, then it would be possible to offer a new approach to the prevention and handling of behavioral problems.

In considering the design of such a program, it was necessary to clarify whether such training would constitute the imposition of middle-class values on children for whom such values may be inappropriate. Chilman (1966) has in fact stated that competence, intellectual achievement, and impulse control as criteria for positive mental health may only reflect a middle-class value orientation. She suggests that the constant and overpowering frustrations of the slum-dweller make him take a pragmatic, physically aggressive, impulsive, and alienated view of life. Results of studies of problem-solving capacity as a measure of adjustment indicate that indeed, among normal youngsters, more lower-class children create pragmatic, impulsive, and physically aggressive strategies than do middle-class children.

However, Chilman's statement (1966, p. 30) that in the lower class "a more goal-committed, rationalistic, involved, and verbal approach might lead to higher rates of mental breakdown than now occur" is not supported by the evidence. At all socio-economic levels (and ages) we found that well-adjusted people have not only a greater number of options but also a wider range of rational, thoughtful, and nonaggressive options than do the poorly adjusted. The well-adjusted individual irrespective of social class or economic level may be one who can weigh the possibilities and decide, for instance, whether physical or nonphysical retaliation to a verbal attack is more appropriate or effective for him at a given moment. The better problem-solver fails less often in getting what he wants and thus proves to be more competent, have greater self-esteem, and be less likely to suffer from unpleasant (symptomatic) feelings and maladaptive behaviors. This is true of slum-dwellers as well as the privileged.

The purpose of any such program is thus to bring the cognitive interpersonal problem-solving skills and subsequent behavioral adjustment of four-year olds deficient in those areas up to the level of efficient youngsters of the same age who face the same social and interpersonal problems. Value judgments are not placed on thoughts of hitting or saying please or planning ahead. Hitting is in fact one solution to a variety of problems. It is the ability to think of hitting as well as other ways of handling a situation and the consequences of each that seems to be most relevant to personal adjustment.

Basic Principles

The structured training program for young children has an underlying approach: to teach children how to think, not what to think. The aim is to help the child develop a problem-solving style that will guide him in coping with everyday problems. Seven inter-related principles of teaching make up this approach.

The first principle is prerequisite skills. Children are taken through a series of games to enhance language and thinking skills judged as prerequisite to the final problem-solving skills to be learned. It seems reasonable to assume that a basic ingredient in the ability to think in terms of alternatives in a problem situation is the ability to think with the word *or*. It also seems reasonable to assume that understanding of negation is important in deciding for action in a problem situation because one must often appreciate why *not* do something in the act of deciding in favor of something else. The word *not* is taught as an aid to understanding the concept of nega-tion. In addition the word *and* is important if children are to learn to think in terms of more than one aspect of a situation at a time. It is often useful to encompass the multiple attributes of a situation or person before deciding on action. As other educators such as Bereiter and Englemann (1966) have found, and as we soon dis-covered, many four-year-old youngsters do not have a real under-standing of such words as *and, or,* and *not* even though they use them. Considering the aim of this program, it is necessary to ensure their mastery of such words beforehand.

Other basic language skills taught at the beginning of the program are needed for later lessons, among them the words *some, same,* and *different.* These words are helpful in teaching a later pre-requisite skill to problem-solving, that of being aware of other peo-ples' preferences (for example, *different* people like *different* things; *some* people like apples and some do not; not everybody likes the *same* thing). A child may come to understand that another child might not want to do the same things that he does. Such under-standing may help him avoid coming to faulty conclusions in interpersonal relations. He could recognize, for example, that another child might not want to build with blocks but that he would in fact play with him if he could interest him in an activity he likes. Along the same lines perhaps the other child does like to build with blocks but had done so earlier in the day and would like to do something different now. Using these language tools the children are also taught the notion that the *same* child likes to do different things at different times.

Closely associated with the recognition of individual preferences is sensitivity to the way other people feel, especially the feelings *happy, sad,* and *mad.* What makes one person feel happy may *not* make another person feel happy. In deciding for action it is also important to recognize what action might make another feel sad or angry. Early lessons thus aim at enhancing the child's appreciation of these words and their referents. Also inherent in the lessons about individual preferences and emotions is the notion that there is more than one way to find out what people like and how they feel in different situations. Lessons center on listening to people, watching people, and ways to talk to others to find things out about them.

The second basic principle is that it is easier to teach new concepts with words already familiar to the child. Because almost every child is able to identify the difference between a boy and a girl, the early language games are designed around the words *boy* and *girl:* "Are you a boy *or* are you a girl? Johnny is a boy. Johnny is *not* a ————." All children studied could recognize a flower and a hat, so flowers and hats are used to teach the word *not* ("Johnny has a flower. He does *not* have a hat.") and to teach the words *same* and *different* ("A hat is *different* from a flower. A hat is *not* the *same* as a flower."). To teach about individual preferences, the teaches uses pictures of animals, different kinds of food, and forms of transportation that can all be identified. We assume that using familiar content not only helps teach new concepts but also gives the child a sense of comfort and accomplishment from the very beginning.

The third principle is that content and situations center around people rather than objects and around interpersonal relations rather than impersonal problems (such as solving a puzzle). Thus the words *boy* and *girl,* not *tin can* and *pencil,* were chosen for the first games. The flowers and hats, although objects, are placed in a context of awareness and watching of other people. Instead of asking whether a hat is or is not a flower, the objects are given to the children, who have to notice which objects they have or do not have and which objects other children have or do not have. Watching other children (or the teacher) is necessary for many lessons: "Johnny is patting his head. Sally is stamping her foot. Patting our head and stamping our foot are *not* the *same*. Johnny is doing something *different* than Sally." Pictures of animals, food, and transportation are used to teach that different children like different things, not to teach about different kinds of animals, foods, and forms of transportation. The notion of finding and gathering information not already known is adapted from the teaching techniques of Bereiter and Englemann, but instead of using inanimate objects (for example, whether a juice can is hot or cold) the focus is on how to find out about other people's preferences and emotions.

The fourth principle of the program is the emphasis on learning and understanding a concept rather than using specific words or complete sentences. For example the word *not* is taught to guide the child in his thinking, but the important concept to be learned is that of negation. Therefore a child's statement "I don't like no apples" is just as acceptable as "I do not like apples." We feel that our approach is justified because it was the total number of different ideas that related to behavioral adjustment in our research, not the ways in which they were expressed. In the research studies mentioned, a child received the same credit for "I ain't got no trucks" as for "I do not have any trucks."

The fifth principle emphasizes teaching the child the habit of seeking solutions and evaluating them on the basis of their potential consequences. No emphasis is placed on the absolute merits of a particular solution to a problem. If a child offers "hit him" as a solution to getting a bike from another child, the teacher says: "That's one idea. What might happen next if you hit him?" After the child evaluates his idea (whether it is less socially acceptable such as "hit him" or more socially acceptable such as "ask him"), he is asked if he can think of a different idea.

To help the child learn to evaluate his alternative solutions, additional prerequisite skill words *maybe* and *might* are taught, and there are exercises in the concepts of *why-because* and statements of *if-then* logic. The assumption is that the words *maybe* and *might* help one to evaluate solutions in light of potential or probable consequences to an act (for example, "If I hit him, he *might* hit me back."). The effect of an act on another person is never a certainty, and the words *maybe* and *might* help to teach the child to select actions based on alternative consequences (for example,

"If I hit him he *might* hit me back *or* he *might* not be my friend.").
Inherent in this style of thinking is also the *if-then* logic.

As a prerequisite to consequential thinking, the *why-because* connectives are taught because our research suggests a relationship between causal thinking, consequential thinking, and ability to conceptualize alternative solutions to problems. It seems reasonable to assume that a child who can recognize that another child may have hit him *because* he hit him first would have a greater understanding of consequences to an act and be able to evaluate the utility of hitting the next time around.

Teaching a child how to think so that he can evaluate his solutions contrasts with the approach taken by others. Holzworth (1964) taught youngsters "socially acceptable" ideas. If a child offered "grab" as a way to obtain a toy, Holzworth asked: "Will Jimmy act nicely toward you if you just grab the fire engine? Will Jimmy act nicely toward you if you ask him nicely if you can play with it?" Holzworth's results indicate that physically aggressive and grabbing behaviors in the classroom did not improve significantly; we speculate that one reason could be that the child was simply told the merits of his idea and not encouraged or taught how to evaluate them himself.

The sixth principle of this program stresses that the child think of and evaluate his own ideas and that he be encouraged to offer his ideas in the context of problem situations. This principle is based on the assumption that a child is more likely to act on a conclusion if he has come upon it himself than if he is offered a solution by someone else. In the training program the child is asked for his own ideas and his own evaluation of what he sees as possible consequences.

Attempts to alter behavioral adjustment by altering thought processes (see Giebink, Stover, and Fahl, 1968; Meichenbaum and Goodman, 1971) have taken a different approach by directly telling the child what to say or do. The fact that behavioral change did not generalize to other situations (see Meichenbaum and Goodman's study) may be due in part to the fact that the children did not learn how to generate their own thoughts. It is likely that children of all ages adjust across a range of situations when they acquire tools of thought that are useful and applicable from situation to situation.

The seventh and final principle of the program is that the cognitive problem-solving skills and all the prerequisite concepts are not taught as ends in themselves but as antecedent, mediating skills necessary to enhance behavioral adjustment, reduce maladaptive behaviors (such as impulsivity, overemotionality, overinhibition in the classroom), and help the young child acquire behaviors through which he can function successfully with his peers and adults.

This focus distinguishes our program from most early training programs designed essentially to enhance cognitive and linguistic functioning. The purpose of these programs, most of them designed for disadvantaged preschool children (see Grotberg, 1969; Fein and Clarke-Stewart, 1973), has been to increase IQ scores and scores on general tests of cognitive functioning or to enhance language or perceptual skills. Not all these programs ignore the social and emotional well-being of the child as goals. In fact Caldwell (1967) makes the point that optimal learning environments for young children should encompass both purely cognitive and emotional goals. But as Bronfenbrenner (1973) points out the main focus of these programs is on general cognitive development per se, which has perhaps led to an undervaluation of emotional and social outcomes.

Deriving from this difference in focus is a second feature that distinguishes our program. The cognitive skills selected for training were chosen on the basis of their specific relationship to the social adjustment of the child. The focus on enhancing the ability of young children to imagine solutions and consequences to real-life problems was dictated by research demonstrating a relationship between this ability and social adjustment irrespective of a child's general level of cognitive ability (measured IQ). Further, our evaluation research (see Chapter Seven) demonstrated that social adjustment improves if these skills are enhanced.

What distinguishes our program is thus that neither its social adjustment goal nor its cognitive training means is considered in isolation. Certain cognitive processes are viewed as mediating behavioral adjustment, and the aim of research and the program has been to use these processes for improving social adjustment and avoiding maladjustment.

In summary the seven fundamental principles in the design of the training program to be presented are as follows.

(1) To teach prerequisite language and thinking skills before teaching problem-solving strategies.

(2) To teach new concepts in the context of familiar content.

(3) To base program content on people and interpersonal relations rather than objects and impersonal situations.

(4) To teach generally applicable concepts rather than correct grammar.

(5) To teach the habit of seeking solutions and evaluating them on the basis of their potential consequences rather than the absolute merits of a particular solution to a problem.

(6) To encourage the child to create his own ideas and offer them in the context of the problem.

(7) To teach problem-solving skills not as ends in themselves but in relation to the adaptiveness of overt behavioral adjustment.

Creation of the Program Script

The final program script presented in Chapter Eleven was developed over a three-year period, each year calling for revision on the basis of experience gained in working with groups of children.

During the first year the lessons were presented to the children by the research staff to gain first-hand knowledge of how the children would respond. After each lesson the research staff discussed the day's activities. As a result of long and detailed discussions about how well the lessons were attended to and understood, several lessons were changed, new prerequisite skills were added, and a number of other refinements were made.

An early question was whether the program should be presented as formal lessons or as games. After initial trials with a group of six children it was decided that presentation in the form of games was more effective. During this period it was also confirmed that some children did not understand the meaning of such words as *and, or,* and *not.*

After a few weeks of initial experimentation the entire program was presented to a different group of children, now totaling twenty-two, divided into small groups and taken out of their class-rooms. It was discovered that in the early games, designed to teach how to gather information about people, the children were not able to understand the notion that "watching what they do" and "listening to what they say" were two such ways. They could not understand, for example, that one way to realize another person is feeling sad is to see that he is crying. Another way is to hear him crying. Several games were devised to emphasize that "we can see with our eyes *and* we can hear with our ears." These games had to be redesigned to cover a longer period of time than originally planned. If a child correctly identified another as being sad "because he's crying," he was then asked, "How can you tell he's crying?" It was also realized that by calling these games the How Can You Tell? games it was easier to focus attention on the concepts to be taught. Through many exercises added to the script, the children seemed to become aware that one can see someone cry or hear someone cry.

During the first year we realized we were assuming that children had concepts they did not in fact have. In certain games the children were asked to choose between two animals they liked best. When it was pointed out that different children choose different things, however, many youngsters did not understand the word *different*. We then decided to backtrack and include games that teach the meaning of *same* and *different* before using these words in later games.

The way in which questions were asked of the children in certain games also had to be reworked. Initially the children were shown pictures of two animals, say, a dog and a cat, and were asked, "Who would be more happy with a dog?" and "Who would be more happy with a cat?" Instead of being able to point out individual preferences, most children raised their hands to both choices. The questioning was then changed to: "If you could choose a dog *or* a cat to play with, and you could choose only one, which one would you choose?" If the child still chose both, he was told "You can *not* choose the dog *and* cat. You can choose only one, the dog *or* the cat." Only then did it become possible to point out that some children would choose the dog and some would choose the cat and that different children would choose different things.

Because puppet stories were popular, new stories using

puppets were created and added to the script. Besides the stories that we created, stories from children's books were adapted and expanded to fit the script. Some stories proved to be too complicated or too long and were omitted. At times experience with the script indicated that too much time was being given to a particular element. For instance, in the final problem-solving section an attempt was made to elicit alternative solutions and alternative consequences to the same problem over a period of several days. The staff discovered that by the third day the children were no longer interested in talking about the same problem, and the goal was lost. It was decided at that point to condense this section into two days per problem.

During the second year four teachers were trained to use the revised script in their own classrooms. Weekly meetings were held during which the teachers discussed the successes and failures of the preceding week. They were encouraged to offer their own suggestions for changing the presentation of the lessons. One suggestion improved the game dealing with seeing with our eyes and hearing with our ears. It was suggested that the teacher put a book over her face and laugh so that the children could hear but not see her laugh. Then she would remove the book and laugh again. Now the children could experience the sensation of hearing but not seeing a person laugh and of hearing and seeing a person laugh. The children enjoyed this game and took part by putting books over their own faces. From that point on it was much easier to teach the concept that there is more than one way to find out how another person feels.

Games that proved too difficult or did not hold the children's interest had to be changed. For example, in a Why-Because game an animal puppet was used to ask children why his friend would not play with him. This was very successful. However, the question "Can you guess *why* I like snow?" did not elicit a sufficient variety of response to be useful. It was decided to substitute questions with more interesting content, and this elicited a greater number of ideas. ("I like birthday parties. Can you guess *why* I like birthday parties?" "Johnny is not in school today. Can you guess *why* Johnny is not in school today?").

In a game teaching the concept of fairness, the original

lessons involved a story about a child who wanted to take two trips to the zoo even though there was only room in the car for those who did not go on the first trip. A teacher suggested that instead of just talking about fairness it might help to involve the children in simple role-playing. Chairs were used to make a car, and half the group pretended to go to the zoo, imitating the sounds of animals they saw. Then the second group would go on the trip, and the group would talk about whether it would be fair for the same child to go on the trip two times when he could see that there was room for only those who did not go the first time. Each child now seemed to experience the effect of the concept being taught: that someone else would not be able to go on the trip if he had two turns.

We also realized that some concepts from earlier games were not being used by the children in later games and thus needed to be reintroduced later on. A game using finger puppets was developed in which one character was depicted as sad, and lessons to teach sensitivity to others' feelings were repeated. Other games played earlier in the program were also included in the story by having one character ask *why* he is so sad and asking the children for different ways to make him feel happy again. Inherent in this game was also the notion that different people like different things. The first child might offer "give him some candy." The child was then asked (by the character) if *he* liked candy. If the child said yes the character would then say: "Candy does not make me happy." The children would then be asked for a different idea. This procedure, developed for reviewing earlier games, seemed to hold the children's interest for two reasons. First the old concept was presented in a different context through the use of finger puppets (used for the first time); second the children had familiarity with the concept. It was clear from the way they beamed and shouted out ideas that they felt good about using their own ideas.

In the third year the program was conducted on a larger scale with ten teachers being trained to present the script to their classes. Further changes were made. Teachers reported two instances where a child's response to a game could productively become part of the game. In one instance a child initiated the phrase "do you like?" to find out other children's preferences. He kept repeating the phrase every time he asked a question. Soon the other children in the group asked "Do you like ————?" whenever they wanted to know another's preference. Subsequently other teachers suggested this phrase to teach that people differ in their preferences, and the phrase greatly facilitated communication. In fact these games came to be called the Do You Like? games.

In a later game related to the same topic, a teacher showed the children a picture with a watermelon, grapes, oranges, apples, and bananas. After the children stated their preference (which was all the script at that time asked for) one child shouted, "I do *not* like grapes!" "I do *not* like bananas!" The teacher then asked which fruits she did like. After each fruit in the picture was named, the teacher repeated: "Do you like bananas?" The child again said no, indicating to the teacher that she really understood the negation. The notion of testing the child's understanding of the negation was instituted by the other teachers and proved to be fun for the children and valuable to the teachers when they discovered which children responded inconsistently.

Regarding program content, changes had to be made in the final problem-solving section. To increase interest in the problems, attention was given to only one facet of problem-solving per problem; that is, either eliciting alternative solutions or alternative consequences but not both. In this way only one day was given to each problem. To enhance interest and provide variety, other games were presented after three or four problems to avoid twelve successive days of problem situations.

Teacher instructions in the problem-solving section were rewritten for clarity with complete descriptions of how to elicit ideas and how to redirect the children's ideas when they became irrelevant.

Another general area of improvement was the development of stage cues or footnotes in the script designed to help the teacher elicit maximum response from the children. The research staff periodically watched training sessions and sometimes offered suggestions based on these observations. If these suggestions and others offered by the teachers were agreed to be effective, they were incorporated into the script.

Certain general techniques of teaching were found to be effective during development of the script. We discovered that the pace had to be kept relatively rapid to hold the children's interest and inspire them to respond and pay attention. Allowing each child to take the role of leader after the concepts taught in the games have been mastered not only seems to give the child a sense of importance but also helps to reinforce the concepts learned.

It became increasingly evident, especially in the second and third years, that at times children give seemingly irrelevant or inappropriate responses to questions or problem situations. In response to how a boy playing ball with another boy might feel, most children agreed that he was probably feeling happy. One child said, "He is sad." At first the teacher thought the child still did not understand the difference between happy and sad. Instead of correcting him, however, the teacher asked him why he thought the boy might be sad. The child replied, "The ball might hit him in the eye." In response to a problem dealing with how a boy can get a fireman to give him a ride on the firetruck, a child said, "Look in his mommy's pocketbook." When asked how that could get him a ride, he answered, "Then he can give him the money." All the children could evaluate this solution. Had the child not been questioned further his idea might have been regarded as irrelevant. Both these examples point out the importance of questioning a child who gives an apparently irrelevant answer or one that is opposite to expectation.

In games designed to elicit different ideas, after a child gave an answer the teachers learned not to follow immediately with the question, "Does anyone have a different idea?" The first child may feel that his answer was not a good one. It is more effective to follow up with: "That's one idea. Now the idea of this game is to think of lots of different ideas. Can anyone think of a different idea?" In this way the first child knows that he is part of the game and that his idea is not being rejected in the teacher's quest for a new idea.

The script given in Chapter Eleven has gone through many changes. No claim is made for its being the best script possible. However, much attention has been paid to its sequencing, the interest level of its elements, and its feasibility. In its present form teachers can learn to use it and enjoy working with it. Moreover its application has been shown to alter the thinking and consequently the behavioral adjustment of the children involved.

3

Outline of the Training Program Script

The training program follows a script composed of daily lessons in game form. This script is divided into two sections—prerequisite skills and problem-solving skills—and incorporates techniques for training, for maintaining interest, and for eliciting responses from the children. Based on three years of research and revision described earlier, the script indicates the proper sequencing and the time needed to teach the skills.

The formal training takes nine or ten weeks of daily instruction. For maximum attention and responsiveness the initial daily sessions should last about five minutes, reaching a maximum of twenty minutes within three or four weeks. The training program style may be employed during the remainder of the day as occasion arises (see Chapters Five and Six).

It has been found best to work with the children in small

groups of from six to eight, some boys and some girls. Because the style of the program requires the children to initiate much of the conversation through guided dialogues, the group should be composed of both responding and nonresponding children since the former are a great help to the latter.

During training it is unimportant whether the children sit on the floor or on chairs. If chairs are used they should be placed in a semicircle, not a straight line. The teacher should have the quiet youngsters sit near the center of the group. If the group is sitting on the floor the quiet children should be in front, as close to the pictures as possible.

The script need not be followed word for word, and it is not necessary to memorize the dialogues. The teacher may read from the script on her lap by casually looking down at it.

In the program script, each day as well as the games to be played are numbered. The day numbers are only approximate guidelines. Some groups can absorb more than others on a given day, and the teacher can complete more or less than indicated depending on the group's reactions and readiness to move on. It is important, however, that the teacher stop for the day when the group gets restless. Experience suggests that lessons should be repeated only if absolutely necessary. Though children respond enthusiastically to the materials and games the first time through, they show less interest in some of them the second time. Because the games are sequenced there is opportunity for a concept not mastered in a particular game to be learned in later games.

Whenever possible the classroom aide (if available) should sit in with the group and keep the disruptive children near her. She can participate in the lesson whenever necessary to help maintain interest and can occasionally encourage the inhibited children to whisper in her ear. Because only part of the class is being trained at a time, however, the aide may often have to be with the other children during formal training. If possible the aide should conduct formal training occasionally so that she, as well as the teacher, is aware of the style and goals of the program.

The materials consist of novelty trinkets, pictures, storybooks, animal puppets, and finger puppets chosen to fit the needs and goals of the program. The materials are simple so that they can be easily substituted or even constructed if they are unavailable or too expensive.

Prerequisite Skills

The script includes a detailed day-by-day description of the training program including dialogue, games and interpersonal procedures, and cues to the teacher regarding technique. Each game has a specific goal. The intent at this point is to outline the content and rationale of the games and briefly to describe examples of them. The complete script and a list of materials are presented in Chapter Eleven.

Games 1 to 7: Language, Listening, and Paying Attention. Certain basic concepts are necessary for seeing alternative solutions and their consequences as well as for understanding the meaning of the problem. Solving a problem includes deciding on solution A *or* B, A *and* B, and A but *not* B. Bereiter and Englemann (1966), in their book *Teaching Disadvantaged Children in the Preschool,* found that many four-year-old children attending nursery school do not know the meaning of the words *and, or,* and *not.* The early games and techniques in our curriculum have been adapted from the language curriculum of Bereiter and Englemann but with the focus on interpersonal relationships. In our program, unlike that of Bereiter and Englemann, the child is not drilled to use specific words or told what to say.

The goal is to teach children to use these language skills as a tool to solve interpersonal problems, imagine alternatives (*or*), and consider the negation (*not*). The first game teaches the concept *is* by simply pointing out that Johnny *is* a boy and Mary *is* a girl. In this game it is important that the children pay attention because they must tap their knees if the teacher points to a boy and raise their hands if she points to a girl. Besides requiring the children to listen, the movement maintains interest. To introduce the concept *not,* the teacher points out that Johnny *is* a boy. Johnny is *not* a girl. The next day the children have fun with the word *not* by naming silly things they are not. To maintain interest the children are given objects (such as hats and flowers) and asked who is and who is not holding a flower. To encourage the children to become aware of others they are also asked what another child is and is not holding.

The words *same* and *different* are important in naming new and different alternatives and in being able to discriminate between them in solving problems. One of the most effective and best liked games to teach these concepts, keeping the focus on people rather than objects, is to have the children perform various movements with their bodies. Sometimes a child does the same thing as the teacher (such as patting her head) and sometimes the group is asked to do something different from what the teacher is doing. This game not only requires the children to think about the words *same* and *different* but also provides another opportunity to think about what other people are doing. These concepts are also taught with objects, and the children are asked such questions as "Is a hat the *same* as a flower *or* are they *different?*"

Games 8 to 10: Identifying Emotions—Rudiments of Logic. To consider people's emotions in problem-solving it is necessary to be able to identify them. Pictures and demonstrations of such expressions as laughing and crying are used for this purpose. *If-then* statements teach children to reason in terms of cause and effect and appreciation of consequences (*If* it is daytime, *then* it is *not*————.").

Game 11: Multiple Attributes (and-not). In problem-solving it is necessary to be aware that there is more than one element to consider about a person before taking action. This game is a step toward teaching this awareness ("This girl is clapping *and* she is marching *and* she is ————.").

Games 12 to 14: How Can We Tell? After having mastered the word-concepts the children focus on pre-problem-solving skills. With an understanding of words that designate feeling—*happy, sad, mad*—it is possible to learn that different people feel differently, that feelings change, and that it is possible to find these things out by listening, watching, and asking. Attending to others' feelings and preferences is an important element in later problem-solving ability, including consequential thinking. Exercises are conducted so that the child cannot see (the leader's face is covered with a book) but can hear that the leader is happy by her voice and her laugh.

Dialogues about what ears and eyes can and cannot do are included.

That everybody does not choose the same thing is also an important concept. Young children frequently assume that others would choose what they choose, which leads to faulty conclusions in interpersonal relations. Nor can a child assume, for example, that because a doll made A happy a doll would also make B happy. Pictures of foods, forms of transportation, places, and the like are shown, each child indicates his choice (for example, of a dog or cat), and individual preferences are pinpointed. These games offer guidance on how to find out what other people like, and the children take an active role in doing the asking. Throughout these games the point is made that different people like different things and that this is all right.

Games 15 and 16: Do You Like? A phrase children enjoy using to find out other people's preferences is "Do you like ———?" Beyond the ability to identify emotions is the need to be sensitive to other people's feelings in problem-solving ("Let's pretend we know that Sally likes candy. If Janie let her have a piece of candy, would that make Sally happy? How would Sally feel if Janie would not let her have a piece of candy?").

Game 17: Why-Because Connectives. In understanding the effect of one's behavior on another and of others' behavior on oneself, the concept of causality is important. The *why-because* connective is important in evaluating solutions to an act ("He hit me *because* I hit him first.") as well as in situations where a problem could be avoided (" I fell *because* I ran too fast.").

A picture the children particularly like shows a girl having fallen off her bike and crying, and a boy standing near her. First the children are asked "How does this girl feel?" and then "How can you tell?" Next the children are asked why she might have fallen off her bike, followed by "How can this boy make the girl feel *happy* again?"

The Why-Because games also aid the teacher in communicating with the children. Sometimes a child responds with a seemingly irrelevant answer but when asked why may reveal a relevant thought after all. When one child said that a girl would be happy while sick in bed, the teacher at first thought he did not understand the concept *happy*. When asked why the girl might be happy, however, the child responded, "Mommy brings me presents."

Game 18: More about Individual Preferences. In this game the emphasis is again on finding out what other people like and on the fact that different people like different things, utilizing language concepts previously learned. The concept *not* is used by asking a child what he does *not* like. If he says he likes apples, oranges, and bananas but not grapes, the teacher repeats "Do you like apples? Do you like oranges? Do you like bananas? Do you like grapes?" If the child answers yes to the first three and no to grapes, the teacher can assume that the child has mastered the *not* concept.

Also stressed is the notion that another person may be happy about an experience that the child himself might not be happy about, such as being sick in bed. The children are encouraged to express any emotions they wish about an event and are always asked why they feel the way they do about an event.

Game 19: A Story. The story *Will I Have a Friend?* (Cohen, 1967) is read with specific questions interpersed to review previously learned concepts about emotions. For example, the story is interrupted at one point with the following: "Jimmy really wants a friend. Nobody wants to play with him. How does Jim feel? Why do you think he feels ————?"

Game 20: What Might Happen Next? In learning to think of consequences that may ensue from an act, the words *maybe, why,* and *because* become important. Again emphasis is placed on *if-then* statements and on the fact that emotions are important consequences. For example, "Let's pretend Kevin scribbled on Karl's painting . . . you know, so Karl could not draw on it anymore. How might Karl feel? Why might Karl feel ————? Because ————." The concepts of causality (*why-because*) and the notions of *might* and *maybe* become important throughout the pre-problem-solving lessons. These words help when considering solutions in light of potential consequences of an act ("If I hit him, he *might* hit me back.") and in recognizing that the effect of an act on another person or oneself is never a certainty.

Game 21: Puppet Story. The puppet story was created to stimulate thinking about emotions and how to cope with varying emotions. The first part of the story finds the main character (Allie the Alligator) very sad because he cannot run and play with the other alligators. It is pointed out to him that he can do other things even better than the other alligators, and the story ends with Allie very happy. The second part of the story (presented on a new day) is an illustrated problem-solving situation, stressing three kinds of thought. First, one cannot assume that because an individual likes something he will like it all the time; the same individual likes different things at different times. (Allie does not like to swim all the time.) Second, one must gather information and not come to a hasty conclusion. (Whipple the Whale thought Allie did not want to play with him because Allie did not want to go swimming at that moment.) Third, it is often important to find out what the other individual likes in order to solve an interpersonal problem.

Game 22: Review. The concepts How Can I Find Out?, Do You Like?, and How Can You Tell? are reviewed with games that focus on discovering the preferences of others.

Game 23: More Why-Because. In this game a puppet tells the children, "I'm very hungry." The children are encouraged to ask him why. After several such statements the game is changed and the puppet tells the children to make up the *because* to such statements as "I like birthday parties." After one reason is given, the puppet asks for a different *because*.

Game 24: Lessons in Fairness. Based on previous research (Shure, 1968), concepts of fairness understood by four-year olds are included. The concept is based on the proposition that in an equal situation, where two individuals do not differ in their right to an object, the fair solution is for both to receive equal benefit from that object. Acquisition of this concept is meant to provide each child with some conception of the rights of others as an element in decision-making and to be sensitive to the emotions of others. For example: "I have a raisin here for each of you and I'm going to let each of you take one. If Johnny takes two raisins, then someone will not have any raisins. Is that *fair?*"

Game 25: More Fairness. Inherent in this game is the notion that sometimes, in being fair, it is necessary to wait. Only some children can go on the first car ride because the car does not have enough room for everyone. Fairness resides in the fact that a child who goes on the ride the first time cannot go the second time and still be fair.

Problem-Solving Skills

After having mastered the word-concepts and pre-problem-solving skills, the children are ready for the games and dialogues that teach interpersonal problem-solving skills. The two goals of these games are to get the children to think of alternative solutions to hypothetical problems and to encourage them to appreciate consequences. In eliciting solutions and consequences the children are guided through appropriate dialogues, but in keeping with the principles guiding the style of the program they are never told a particular solution or consequence.

The problem-solving portion of the script is divided into three sections: alternative solutions, alternative consequences, and the pairing of solutions with their potential consequences.

In eliciting alternative solutions, pictures that depict a problem situation are placed on a blackboard. In one picture a child and her mother are in a grocery store and the children are told, "This girl wants her mother to buy her a box of cookies." They are then asked what the girl might do or say so that her mother will buy her the cookies. In guiding these games the teacher uses the basic word-concepts taught earlier as probing techniques. After one idea is given, the teacher follows with: "That's one idea. Now the idea of this game is to think of lots of *different* ideas, lots of *different* ways the girl can get her mother to buy her the cookies." After another idea is offered, the teacher says: "She can (*repeats the first idea*) or she can (*repeats the second idea*). Who can think of a new, *different* idea?" Other examples include one child wanting another to sit down so he can see the storybook, one child wanting another to help him put the toys away, and a girl wanting a lady to read her a story. In addition to pictures, a problem is presented simulating a real-life experience. Each child is given an animal trinket and asked if he can think of a way to get another child to let him play with the one he wants. In these games any relevant solution to a problem is accepted, including forceful ones such as hit, snatch, and the like.

In the second section the teacher elicits alternative consequences to an act and the children evaluate each consequence for themselves. The teacher-guided dialogues use many of the prerequisite tools. A sample problem is, "This boy wants this girl to let him feed the animals." After one solution is given ("push her out of the way"), the children are asked "What *might* happen next if he pushes her out of the way?" After one response is given ("push him back"), the teacher follows with: "That's one thing that *might* happen. If he pushes her, *then* she might push him back. Who can think of something *different* that might happen? She might push him back *or* she might———." The teacher also asks, "What might the girl do or say if he pushes her?"

After several possible consequences are offered, the teacher asks: "Who thinks pushing her out of the way is a good idea? Who thinks pushing her out of the way is not a good idea?" Each child is then asked why he thinks it is or is not a good idea: "*Because*———." If a statement involving feelings is not offered, the teacher asks: "How *might* the girl feel if he pushes her out of the way?" The children are encouraged to evaluate such solutions as "ask him" or "say please" in the same manner they are encouraged to evaluate solutions that involve force. Asking may not always be judged a good idea, as many children have pointed out, because the girl might say no. Other pictures include a teacher looking at one child's painting while another child wants her to look at his picture. As is true of the games to elicit alternative solutions, four situations are presented through pictures, each on a separate day.

Interspersed between problems is *The Circus Baby* (Petersham and Petersham, 1950), a story well suited to stimulate talk about emotions and problem situations. Also interspersed is a review game using wooden finger puppets that tell a story similar to that of "Allie the Alligator" discussed previously.

The final section of the script involves the pairing of solutions and consequences; the goal is to teach a child to think of a solution and then immediately of its possible consequence, followed by another solution and its likely consequence. The process is repeated until pairs are no longer offered. Four situations are presented; one example is a girl on a bike who wants a boy in a wagon to get out of her way so she can pass.

The probing techniques are presented in the body of the script (see Chapter Eleven). It should be pointed out that the problems presented in the pictures are for the most part fabricated. Although in one picture a child is shown to be clearly in the way of another child during story time, most pictures do not depict an obvious problem situation. For example, there is no obvious sign that the giry in the grocery store wants her mother to buy her a box of cookies or that the boy wants the girl to let him feed the animals. Any picture of children and an adult can be used; the problem situation can be defined verbally by the teacher when the picture is presented. The child in the picture can want something from the adult or other child in the picture such as cookies, to be read a story, or simply to play. If two children are shown eating cupcakes, a story can be made up in which one child snatches a cupcake from the other. Such a story can be discussed, for instance, in light of fairness and consequences. Inventing a problem situation from a picture is not a difficult task, and the teacher can make up a variety of her own materials for the program.

Redesign of Script for Kindergarten

The evaluative research design of this program included a follow-up of the preschool youngsters as they moved into kindergarten. During this second year half the first-year training group again received the special problem-solving training; the other half served as controls. Half the first-year control group received training at age five; the other half again served as controls. As with the first year of the study, pre- and posttesting of both cognitive and behavioral functioning of all the children was carried out. Analysis of these data have begun (see Chapter Seven), and will indicate whether the program at age four is still effective during the second year or whether it needs a follow-up. It will also be possible to determine whether such a program should begin when the child is four or whether it can begin a year later without loss in efficiency.

In redesigning the program script for kindergarten it was important to consider the needs and abilities of those who were previously exposed to the training and those who would be receiving it for the first time. Although it was judged important to repeat the prerequisite and problem-solving games for the second-year training youngsters, a major consideration was to maintain their interest and enthusiasm in playing the games. In so doing, it was necessary to change the material and problem situations and to add new concepts to the script considering the added sophistication of the children. An important consideration in doing this, however, was to design the games so that they would not be too sophisticated for those receiving training for the first time.

Like the earlier script the kindergarten script is divided into two sections: prerequisite skills and problem-solving skills. New games are described here in some detail because they are not included in the script in Chapter Eleven. The kindergarten script is available from the authors.

The early games concentrate on the basic word-concepts *is, and, or, not, some-all,* and *same-different.* The initial games are similar to those used for the four-year olds except that content is substituted to avoid repetition in the second year. For example, instead of tapping knees when the teacher points to someone who is a boy, the children tap their knees if the teacher points to someone who is sitting on a chair. The not games are introduced by using the child's own name: "Your name *is* Johnny. Your name is *not* Peter. Your name is *not* ———." Once the concept *not* is understood in this context, the teacher sees if a child is paying attention by saying to Robert, "Your name is *not* Robert." The Fun with Not game (Game 4) is repeated as before because children particularly enjoy this game and because it is not too difficult for those receiving training for the first time.

New and sophisticated games using the word *not* have been added and labeled optional. Whether a teacher should carry out a game marked optional must be determined by her judgment of the readiness of the group. One such game is called the Do, Do Not game. The teacher switches between do tap your knee and do not tap your knee, and the children have to pay close attention to what the teacher is saying. A slightly more sophisticated game, also optional, requires special attention from the children: "I'm going to say a word. The word is *head.* Can you show me your *head?* Good,

now if I say *head,* you *do* point to your *head.* I'm going to say lots
of other words too. Like *leg.* But only point to your head if I say
head. If I say *leg, do not* point to your *leg.* Point only if I say *head.*"
The teacher then points to her leg and says: "Good, you did *not*
point to your leg. *Head.* Good, you pointed to your head because I
said *head. Arm.* Good, you did *not* point to your arm because we
only point when I say *head.*"

The game used with the four-year olds, asking who is and
who is not holding a hat, is repeated with animal picture cards instead
of hats. An optional addition is: "Sandra, are you holding a zebra?"
When the child says yes, the teacher continues: "Are you holding
a cow?" When the child says no, the teacher says: "You are holding a zebra. You are *not* holding a cow. Are you *not* holding a zebra
or are you *not* holding a cow?" The animal cards are also used to
teach the word *and:* "Johnny, are you holding a dog *and* a cat or
are you holding a horse *and* a rabbit?"

If-then concepts are introduced next, first at a simple level as
with the four-year olds and then through a difficult optional game
called Who Am I Thinking Of?: "I am thinking of a girl. I am *not*
thinking of a ———. If I am thinking of a girl, who am I *not*
thinking of? Good, I am not thinking of Larry because Larry is a
boy. Who else am I *not* thinking of?" The game continues: "I am
thinking of a girl with a red ribbon in her hair. What girl am I *not*
thinking of?" This questioning continues and then the teacher asks:
"Who *am* I thinking of?" To add to the difficulty of this game
the teacher selects something that two of the children happen to be
wearing, such as red socks. The teacher then says: "I am thinking
of a boy with red socks. What boy am I *not* thinking of?" "Good, I
am *not* thinking of Richard because he does *not* have red socks."
After this line of questioning the teacher continues with: "Tell me,
which boys do have red socks? Yes, David *and* Clarence have red
socks. *If* I am thinking of a boy with red socks, *then* I am either
thinking of David *or* I am thinking of Clarence. Now I am only
thinking of one of them. I am thinking of a boy who has red socks
and a white shirt. Who am I thinking of? Yes, I am thinking of
David because David has red socks *and* a white shirt. What boy has
red socks but *not* a white shirt?

One of the games liked best by the four-year olds is that of changing body movements when learning the concepts *same* and *different*. This game is repeated in the script for five-year olds. In addition pictures of children are shown doing the same and different things. For example, after being told "This boy is walking in the snow, and there is another boy walking in the snow," the children are asked: "Are these boys doing the *same* thing or are they doing something *different?*" The questioning is repeated with several pictures of children doing either the same or different things. In a sequenced series of games children are asked to point to various combinations of the same child doing different things, different children doing the same thing, and different children doing different things.

After feelings are introduced, pictures of children depicting different emotions are included: "Do these children feel the *same* way or a *different* way? Show me a boy who does *not* feel the *same* way as this boy." Besides reinforcing the concepts *same* and *different,* these games illustrate the notion that different children can do different things and feel different ways at different times. Sensitivity to what others are doing and how others are feeling is emphasized throughout the kindergarten script.

The next several games, which teach the concepts *and, if-then,* and finding out about individual preferences, follow essentially the same format as the script for four-year olds except that different pictures and trinkets are used.

A new game, Where Is It? Where Is It Not?, has proved effective. As a way to review basic concepts and encourage attentiveness, this game is a form of the popular game Concentration. Pictures of happy, sad, and angry children are placed on separate boards and then turned around. The children are asked to remember which child is pictured on which board. New pictures are then shown and the group is asked: "Where is a boy who feels the *same* way as this boy?" Sometimes the children are asked: "Where is a boy who feels a *different* way from this boy?" Inserted in this line of questioning is, for example: "Where is the happy boy *not?*" or "Which board is the sad boy on?"

Due to the popularity of the animal puppet stories, both parts of "Allie the Alligator" are repeated in the script for five-year olds, and others have been added. For example, Freddie the Frog wants to hop in the grass but Woofie the Wolf does not. These stories are important because they reinforce use of the important concepts underlying them.

The word-concepts *before-after* and *now-later* are introduced in the kindergarten script. Though used in the script for four-year olds, they are not specifically taught. These concepts are important in developing interpersonal problem-solving skills. For example: "I can play with that toy *later, not now*" or "I can wait till *after* you're finished" or "If you *do not* want to play with me *now, maybe* you will play with me *later*." As in teaching new concepts to the four-year olds, these words are introduced in the context of familiar everyday events: "Robert, I am talking to you *now*. I will talk to Peter *later*."

The *why-because* connectives are taught in essentially the same way as to four-year olds, with a new concept of emotional causality added. Emphasis here is on asking the children why a child in a picture might be feeling happy, sad, or mad and what another child might have done or said to make that child feel the way he does.

Another addition to the kindergarten script is a game derived from techniques applied informally throughout the day with the four-year olds and aimed at guiding them to avoid potential problems. Pictures are shown of children in potentially dangerous situations, such as pulling a cat's tail or standing in front of a moving swing. Dialogues are conducted in which the children are asked (in reference to the swing): "Where are the boys playing? Is that a good place for the boys to play or *not* a good place? Why is that *not* a good place? *Because* ———. What *might happen next* if the boys play in front of the swing?" If the children offer "They might get hit," the teacher follows with: "How do you think the boys *might* feel if the swing hits them?" This line of questioning is used for several such situations. Teaching safety is not the purpose of these games. The aim is to encourage each child to think about what he does and about the potential consequences of his acts for his own feelings and well-being.

The remaining pre-problem-solving games are essentially unchanged except that the words *now-later* and *before-after* are stressed through puppet stories and in the games that teach the concept of fairness.

The problem-solving section is handled in much the same way as with the four-year olds, but new problem pictures are used. Again the problems are not necessarily obvious from the pictures but are defined by what the teacher says about them. In one picture two children are shown with their mother in a grocery store; one child is pushing a grocery cart. The problem presented is: "This girl wants her brother to let her push the grocery cart." In another picture a boy is watching two children at play and the problem presented is: "This boy wants these children to let him play with them." Twelve such problems are presented: four for solutions, four for consequences, and four that pair solutions and consequences.

Finally, pictures with obvious problems are interspersed between problems presented to the children, and the children are asked if they can state the problems by themselves. The goal is to help increase the child's sensitivity to the nature and presence of problems. These pictures come from *My Schoolbook of Picture Stories* (Mill, 1967). In one picture a boy is shown pushing another off a bike; another picture depicts a saw lying in the middle of the floor. These and other pictures are discussed in light of possible solutions and consequences.

Although the research results for five-year olds have not yet been analyzed, it is apparent that those receiving training for the second time show as much enthusiasm for the games as they did the first year. Even though these children had repeated the beginning prerequisite skills, there was no problem in maintaining interest. The old and the new games were well received, and our preliminary judgment is that the program can be presented during two consecutive years without a loss of interest.

4

Implementing the Program with "Difficult" Children

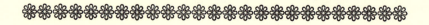

This program has been applied in a variety of classrooms and day-care centers with children who differ widely in temperament, ability, and interpersonal style. Although each child has his own constellation of behaviors reflecting these differences, four kinds of behavior need special attention when they arise during formal training: nonresponding behavior, disruptive behavior, dominating behavior, and "silly" behavior. These behaviors are discussed with suggestions on how to handle them so that the child still benefits from the training.

Nonresponding Behavior

When a teacher is conducting a formal lesson and most of the children are paying attention and responding, it is easy for her to notice them and respond in turn. It is extremely important, however, that she be aware of the child who is sitting in the group but is not participating. Perhaps the child is not participating because he is too shy or hesitant to respond in front of even a small group. Perhaps he prefers not to think about what is going on and is not listening. Perhaps he chooses not to respond in the group because he is not sure he understands what is going on and hesitates to interact. Whatever the reason, his nonresponding is relatively consistent from day to day. Yet a child may decide to be obstinate and remain closed-mouthed even though he normally participates on other days. Sometimes a child may be temporarily upset and not in the mood to play the games. When a child does not respond the teacher must think about the reason because different kinds of nonresponders must be handled in different ways. Certainly the most difficult situations arise with the consistent nonresponder who sits in the group day after day but only plays the role of onlooker. The techniques that follow have been successful only when the teachers have applied them consistently with extreme patience and warmth.

The earliest games in the program script call for little verbalization because they deal primarily with movement, such as raising hands when the teacher points to a girl and tapping knees when the teacher points to a boy. If the child does not react after having been asked, the teacher can simply ask: "Is Johnny a boy?" If he says yes the teacher can say: "Let's tap our knees together because we tap our knees when we point to a boy." If the child remains motionless the teacher can try to encourage him to shake his head to the question "Is Johnny a boy?" If necessary she can follow with "Let's shake our heads together" as she shakes her head dramatically. If the child even barely shakes his head the teacher must shake his hand and say "very good." She has moved the child beyond complete passivity. If the child does not even shake his head after prodding, the issue should be dropped for the moment. Too much pushing may upset the child, and too much time taken with one child may cause the others to become restless and lose interest in the game.

It is generally useful to have consistent nonresponders sit near the teacher or near an aide. An aide sitting with the group can encourage the child to whisper in her ear, a technique that is effective when verbal responses are called for. The important point is that such children should not be further isolated by being allowed to sit in the back apart from the group.

After the word-concept *or* has been introduced it is useful to offer a choice. The child is not asked for long verbalizations but only one-word responses: "Is Johnny a boy *or* is Johnny a girl? Can you tell me, boy or girl?" Sometimes such children are at least willing to say *boy,* the one word asked of them. As soon as consistent nonresponders are willing to respond with one word they are well on their way toward further participating.

In Game 6 (Day 8) the children participate in body movements, doing something the same as the teacher or something different. After several children have played the role of leader a nonresponder may be asked if he would like to be leader. In one instance the child said no. The teacher would not have pressed her, but the child seemed willing to come up to the front. The child put her hand on her head, and the teacher helped her by saying to the group: "Let's do the *same* thing as Tanya." Tanya took such delight in this that she continued her hand motions for several more minutes. The teacher shook her hand vigorously for such leadership. Although Tanya was still not ready to talk, she began laughing much more and from that day on participated in all games involving movement.

For children who are still not responding by the time that games pointing out individual preferences are introduced (Game 14, Day 16), it is feasible to ask them to point to the picture they would choose (such as a dog or a cat). The teacher can try to elicit from the child whether he pointed to a dog or a cat, but even by pointing he is participating.

In any game dealing with emotions the nonresponding child can be encouraged to make a happy (or sad or mad) face, whether at the request of the teacher or together with the teacher. The child can then be asked: "Did you look happy or sad?"

By the time the puppet stories are introduced (Game 21, Day 26) most of the nonresponders are participating, even if only with movement or one-word responses. Once Allie the Alligator has been brought into the group many of these children will begin responding through the puppet. The child can be given the puppet and encouraged to move its mouth while the teacher repeats the story. One child who had not talked at all suddenly responded when the teacher was talking to Allie. After getting used to responding as Allie, the child soon began responding, however slowly, as himself.

Generally when one child parrots another the teacher asks him if he can think of something different, such as a different *because* or something else that might make Sally happy. If a nonresponder parrots another child, however, the teacher should reinforce not what he said but the fact that he said something. She can follow with "Oh, Tommy, you told us too" and shake his hand. In the problem-solving section of the script such children may begin by parroting others when asked for an idea to solve the problem. The child should be allowed to parrot for several days before he is asked to think of a different idea. In the finger puppet story (presented between Problems 8 and 9 in the problem-solving section) the children are encouraged to find out what might make the brother happy. To emphasize the need to find out what will make the brother happy, the character generally says no to the first few guesses. If a child has just begun to respond and offers a guess, however, the brother accepts the first guess and says: "Yes, that would make me happy. Does (*repeating the child's guess*) make you happy?" If the child says yes the brother can say: "We both like the same thing."

Experience suggests that the most severe nonresponder at the outset of the program begins to offer his own ideas after several problems have been presented, even though they may at first be irrelevant. But in line with the style of the program the teacher never gives the child ideas. At most she gives the child a choice, not of solutions but among word-concepts: "Are you happy or are you sad?" Although the child may parrot others such participation is only a stepping-stone to his own thinking skills, which come to fruition after constant daily attention. When the children begin to offer their own different ideas, the beaming expression on their faces is all the teacher needs to reassure her that her consistency, patience, and warmth were well worth the effort.

When a generally responsive child decides to be obstinate and not play, the teacher can try to encourage him to respond by bringing his obstinacy into the game. For example, Benjie decided not to play the same-different game that involved body movement.

He merely sat there. The more the teacher asked him to join in, the more determined he became not to. Then the teacher said to the group: "Raymond is tapping his knee. Sandra is tapping her knee. Are Raymond and Sandra doing the *same* thing or something *different*? Good, they are doing the *same* thing. Tommy is clapping his hands. Benjie is sitting still." Before the teacher could ask the question Benjie jumped up and shouted: "I am not! I'm jumping!" Benjie was now involved.

Sometimes a child in a temporary state of resistance does not respond to the teacher but does respond to another child. Once the Do You Like? game has been introduced (Game 15, Day 19) the teacher can encourage the group to ask the child "Do You Like ———?" When someone discovers something he likes, sometimes the child smiles, feels part of the group, and begins to respond. It is also feasible for the teacher to ask the child, "Are you feeling mad?" If the child says yes the teacher can ask him why. Sometimes he responds and the problem is resolved. If he continues nonresponding the teacher may decide not to push him more that day. In any case she should not insist that he join or leave the group. Such tactics might only begin a negative association with the games, which must be avoided because they are played daily.

Sometimes a child displays a sense of tension or temporary emotional upset and may even turn around, face the other way, and pout. Children who generally respond enthusiastically to the games may, on any given day, demonstrate such behavior. Depending on where the group is in the program script, such behavior can be handled in several ways. One strategy found useful is to engage both the child and the rest of the group in thinking about what that child is doing, treating his behavior as a problem to be solved. The teacher can say: "Is Ralph feeling happy or is he feeling sad? Yes, Ralph is feeling sad. He is not happy. Is he feeling the *same* way as Rachel or a *different* way? Ralph, why are you sad?" If Ralph does not answer, the teacher can ask the group: "Can anyone guess why Ralph is feeling sad? Maybe ———?" If Ralph continues to pout the teacher can follow with: "Can anyone think of a way to help Ralph feel happy?" On one occasion another child began the Do You Like? game with such a pouting classmate, and when asked whether he liked horses the latter turned around and smiled. The teacher got a picture of a horse and asked: "Who does like horses? Who does not like horses? Ralph likes horses. Peter does not like horses. Different children like different things." The teacher continued this only for a minute, Ralph was satisfied, and the game of the day was continued. Whether Ralph was truly upset momentarily or merely seeking attention was irrelevant in the teacher's handling of the situation. Experience with the program suggests that if a child wants attention he can be supplied it through his participation in the program, consistent with the cognitive approach of the training program itself.

Some children become more emotional than usual during the sequence of games dealing with emotions. Although this was not true of most children during our three years of work, those who do may be affected by the fact that emotions are talked about so much. However, such emotional displays are only temporary; once the child can think through his emotions he can in fact cope with them better than before.

Disruptive Behavior

In almost every group there is a child who cannot sit still, goes back and forth from one end of the room to the other, fidgets with any object near him, and in other ways disrupts the group. When placing the group it is best to position such a child away from toys and bookshelves and distracting objects. Allowing children to sit on a covered sandbox only invites the disruptive children to uncover it and play with the sand. Teachers get much better attention when the toys are removed before a lesson. If children are divided into small groups it is better to separate the disruptive children, especially two who happen to be friends.

However, neither our philosophy nor the program demands that children must sit quietly and look at the teacher before a lesson. If the teacher begins the lesson with a fast, exciting pace the group generally settles down because they become interested in what she is saying. If a child continues to be disruptive she can call on him for an idea or have him come up and be the leader. Another technique she can use is similar to that used for the temporary nonresponder. She can focus attention on him by saying: "Albert is doing something *different*. He is playing a *different* game. What is Albert doing?" Such attention is perfectly acceptable and far more effective than threats or saying that the child will have to leave the group if he does not behave. Furthermore such behavior does not become contagious, because each child in the group receives plenty of attention whenever he responds and, as noted earlier, even when he does not.

If a child walks away from the group it is more effective to ignore him than distract the other children. If he is within hearing distance he will generally come back when he hears something that interests him. The severe attention-seeker may leave and come back several times. When he is leader he responds; otherwise he cannot sit still. This child often needs all the attention he can be given outside the formal training until he feels secure enough to join the group and benefit from the program.

Some behaviors that a teacher may consider disruptive can be handled rather easily. One child insisted on sitting on a table in back of the group. The more the teacher demanded that he sit down with the rest of them, the more the child fought back. He was disruptive only because the teacher spent so much time fighting with him. By the time he sat down he was angry and the rest of the group was restless. One day the child shouted out an extremely brilliant idea and gleefully pointed out: "See, I can see the picture from here!" He was paying attention after all. From that day on the teacher recognized that everyone does not have to be sitting in a tight group and that a child may stand back or sit on a table as long as he can play the game. Although it does not usually happen, it is not serious if others follow such a child to the table. In fact they can all sit on the table if they want to, as long as they participate.

Finally, youngsters who often display disruptive behavior during formal training also display impulsive behavior in the classroom. The research data described in Chapter One show that such children, like the inhibited, are deficient in their real-life problem-solving skills. As the program progresses and these children become more adept in their thinking skills, their disruptiveness decreases during the formal training sessions as well as in the classroom. If their motive for disruption is attention-seeking, for example, they now have other, more efficient ways to obtain that attention, ways that make the teacher, and more importantly the child, happy. The style of the program also works for these active children. Their own thoughts are solicited. No one attempts to make them conform by sitting still because many of the games require that the children move about, point to characters on charts, and even act out scenes. Both their thoughts and their physical actions are legitimized as part of the program.

Dominating Behavior

Some children are extremely verbal and have long, drawn-out stories to tell. As soon as the teacher asks a question they are the first to shout out an answer, oblivious to the fact that other children have not had a chance to participate. Without meaning to, such a child dominates the group. Unfortunately the other children do not become involved in that child's stories because they are more interested in what they themselves want to say. As a result the group loses interest and becomes restless, and this stimulates the nonresponder to withdraw and the disruptive child to disrupt.

Such a dominant child has to be handled with care; if the teacher discourages him or stops him he may lose interest. The most effective technique to use with such a child is to allow him to tell his story and explain that "then it will be someone else's turn." This kind of child generally understands and responds to that approach if the discussion is handled with warmth. Using the language of the program the teacher can say: "Denise just had a long turn. Now a *different* child needs a turn." She can focus on the dominating child and ask him: "Who has *not* had a turn? Would you like to pick someone who has not had a chance to tell us a story?" Making the dominating child leader whenever possible is helpful. These techniques are generally all a dominating child needs as long as they are offered in a friendly way. Ignoring him or telling him not to talk so much frustrates and angers him and can lead to withdrawal of interest or disruptive maneuvers on his part.

"Silly" Behavior

Occasionally a child responds with irrelevant or opposite answers or laughs hysterically or makes faces and funny gestures. If a child says that a boy who is crying is happy or that Johnny is a girl, it is sometimes difficult to determine whether he is being silly or whether he in fact does not know the concepts. If the teacher is relatively certain that the child is just being silly she can follow with "Oh, you're just teasing me" and ignore it. If such a child continually parrots another just to be annoying and get attention, the teacher (unlike the case of the nonresponder) can say: "Oh, you can think of a different idea." If the child continues to be silly the teacher should simply ignore him. When he does respond normally she can then give him extra praise and attention, which is probably all he wants. Sometimes a child is silly because he has nothing to contribute, especially in games beyond the prerequisite word-concepts. Such behavior must not be reinforced; rather the teacher should focus his attention on the lessons. As the child develops more thinking skills and has more to contribute, his silliness diminishes.

Before leaving the issue of "difficult" behaviors we must emphasize that games and dialogues usually proceed without major difficulty. Experience indicates that teachers and children enjoy them immensely, probably because the games and materials have been screened for high interest value as well as relevance. Fortunately children who are generally disruptive or dominating do not always act this way. The teacher has plenty of opportunity to engage such children in the program and to praise them for their involvement. The nonresponder is easily brought into the process if he is not pushed to participate too much. Given simple choices, the opportunity to respond minimally at the beginning, and praise for even tentative signs of involvement, the shy child may blossom. Experience and research data indicate that if the teacher is sensitive to these behaviors and is ready to accept and incorporate them and the child into the training process, the program moves smoothly.

5

Informal Use
of the Script

Although each lesson in the formal script has a specific purpose (as described in Chapter Two), the goal of all lessons is to teach the child thinking skills that will increase his chances of success in dealing with real-life interpersonal problems.

To help the child use these cognitive skills in his encounters with peers and figures of authority, the style and techniques of the formal training program may be incorporated into conversations and problem situations as they arise during the remainder of the school day.

The episodes described here actually occurred in training classes and illustrate teacher-guided dialogues consonant with the script style. The dialogues are presented in three major groups: techniques applied during interpersonal conflict or other situations when a child was guided to think things through, make his own decisions, and carry out his own ideas; techniques applied by teachers to help a child avoid potential problems or emotional upset; and ways that the children could be encouraged to use concepts in informal situations throughout the day.

Interpersonal Conflict

Hurting and grabbing behavior. Physical attack such as hitting, kicking, pushing, and grabbing something from another child can be initiated by a child or be a response to his having been attacked or mistreated. The following dialogues illustrate the use of script style in both situations.

In the beginning of the first episode the teacher is talking only to Billy, who wants something that Michael has:

TEACHER: Billy, why did you push Michael off that bike?
BILLY: I want it.
TEACHER: What *might* happen if you push him like that?
BILLY: He might fight.
TEACHER: Is pushing him off a good idea?
BILLY: Yep!
TEACHER: Why?
BILLY: He won't give it to me.
TEACHER: Pushing is *one* way to get that bike. Can you think of a
      different way to get him to let you ride the bike?
BILLY: (*turns to Michael*): Can I have it when you're finished?

This conversation, although carefully guided by the teacher, meets the criteria for the program. First the child (Billy) is communicating at a level at which he is capable. The dialogue utilizes words and concepts that have been taught, such as *not, might,* and *different.* Second, by using these words he is able to do his own thinking. Initially Billy is asked why he pushed Michael off the bike (causal thinking). He is then asked if he thinks that was a good idea in light of his own understanding of what might happen next (consequential thinking). When it is clear that Billy is more interested in getting the bike than in the fact that Michael might fight, the teacher does not tell him what to do. Instead she agrees casually that pushing is one way and then guides him to think of a different solution to the problem (alternative thinking).

In answering Billy's question, "Can I have it when you're finished?", Michael shakes his head yes and the teacher follows it up:

TEACHER: Billy, tell me what you'd like to play with now until Michael is finished with the bike.
BILLY: Nothin'.
TEACHER: Would you like to just do nothing *or* would you like to play with something?
BILLY (*thinks a minute*): A puzzle.
TEACHER: OK, let's go get a puzzle.

The teacher gets Billy involved with a puzzle. This is not a move simply to distract Billy so that he will forget about the bike. Rather she keeps watch on Michael, and when it is clear that Michael has played too long she reminds him that Billy is waiting for his turn. When Michael refuses to give it up the episode continues with the following dialogue:

TEACHER: Michael, is it *fair* for you to play so long with the bike and for Billy *not* to have his turn with it?
MICHAEL: No.
TEACHER: How might Billy feel if you do *not* let him play?
MICHAEL: He won't be my friend.
TEACHER: What can you do to make him feel happy so he will be your friend? Remember, Billy wants a ride on the bike.
MICHAEL (*turns to Billy*): Let's ride together.
TEACHER: Michael, how can you find out if Billy likes that idea?
MICHAEL: Billy, you want to ride with me?
BILLY: Yep! (*And they go riding off together.*)

In this dialogue Michael is asked to think through the situation. The teacher uses additional concepts of the program—such as *fair, happy-sad,* and "How can you find out?"—to encourage taking another's point of view. Although their final solution ends up in Michael's continuing to ride the bike, Billy is satisfied with riding together. Instead of feeling dissatisfaction or frustration the children feel warmly toward each other and good about their own decision.

In another episode Robert grabs some magnets from Erik

and starts hitting him. When Erik hits back Robert begins to cry. Erik has been playing with the magnets for a long time. Robert has been waiting for his turn and needs guidance in finding another solution to getting the magnets. When Robert calms down the teacher asks:

TEACHER: Robert, what happened when you snatched those magnets from Erik?
ROBERT: He hit me.
TEACHER: How did that make you feel?
ROBERT: Sad.
TEACHER: You wanted to play with magnets, right?
ROBERT: Right.
TEACHER: Snatching it is *one* way to get him to give them to you. Can you think of a *different* idea?
ROBERT: Ask him.
TEACHER (*calls Erik over*): Robert, you thought of asking him for the magnets. Go ahead and ask him.
ROBERT (*to Erik*): Can I hold the magnets?
ERIK: No!
TEACHER: Oh, Robert, he said no. Can you think of a *different* way?
ROBERT: (*Starts to cry.*)
TEACHER: I know you're feeling sad now, but I bet if you think real hard, you'll find a different idea. You could ask *or* ————?
ROBERT (*after several seconds*): I'll give 'em back when I'm finished.
ERIK (*reluctantly*): OK.
TEACHER: Very good, Robert. You thought of another way to get Erik to let you play with those magnets. How do you feel now?
ROBERT (*smiles*): Happy.
TEACHER: I'm glad, and you thought of that all by yourself.

Robert is encouraged to continue thinking of alternatives. It is feasible to use the same language used in formal training sessions. With a little guidance and encouragement Robert is able to carry the thought process to completion.

Hitting does not always occur over possession of objects. The next dialogue illustrates a teacher's handling of a situation involving physical retaliation. In this case the teacher sees Stephen hit Darren first:

TEACHER: Darren, why did you hit Stephen?

DARREN: He hit me first.

TEACHER (*brings Stephen over*): Stephen, why did you hit Darren?

STEPHEN: (*Sulks but does not answer.*)

TEACHER: What did Darren do when you hit him?

STEPHEN (*continues sulking but the teacher stays with him.*)

TEACHER: Did Darren go away from your *or* did he hit you back?

STEPHEN (*quietly*): Hit me back. (*The child is more likely to answer if given a choice of simple statements, especially after training sessions using the word "or".*)

TEACHER: Stephen, how do you feel now, happy *or* sad?

STEPHEN: Sad.

TEACHER: Darren, how do you feel now?

DARREN: Mad.

TEACHER: Stephen, you do *not* feel happy. Darren, you do *not* feel happy. Can one of you think of a way to feel happy?

DARREN: Shake hands.

TEACHER: Why is that a good idea?

DARREN: We'll be friends.

TEACHER: Darren, can you ask Stephen if he wants to shake hands?

DARREN: Stephen, do you want to shake hands?

STEPHEN (*Shakes hands vigorously with Darren and they both laugh. For nearly an hour Stephen and Darren chant "we're friends" and insist on sitting next to each other at lunch.*)

In this situation the teacher does not simply stop the hitting or direct the children to stay away from each other or even redirect them by suggesting more constructive activities. She brings both children together and guides them in thinking through the conflict themselves. In this episode, as in the formal training, the child is asked to evaluate his positive ideas just as he is asked to evaluate his negative ones.

When a teacher asks a child why he hit another, the child quite frequently answers "he hit me first." Instead of making an issue of trying to find out who hit first, it may be important to restore positive feelings. Another pair of children responded to a similar dialogue in a different way, incorporating the Do You Like? game (Game 15, Day 19). In this episode Shelly hit Kevin, and now Kevin is crying:

TEACHER: Shelly, why did you hit Kevin?

SHELLY: He hit me first.

TEACHER: How does Kevin feel now?
SHELLY: Sad.
TEACHER: How can you tell he's sad?
SHELLY: He's crying.
TEACHER: What can you do to make him feel happy again?
SHELLY (*turning to Kevin*): Do you like apples?
KEVIN: No.
SHELLY: Do you like bananas?
KEVIN: Yep.
SHELLY (*picking up a block*): Here's a banana.

Both children laughed and for quite a while built a grocery store with blocks. At first they would not let any other children join in their play, which the teacher allowed because of Shelly and Kevin's need to work together.

The problem situations presented in the formal training are similar to real-life problems in the classroom. One of these problems deals with a group of children at story time when one child wants another to sit down so that he can see. At an actual story time, when Bennie wanted Yvette to sit down he pushed her and said, "I can't see." In the following dialogue the teacher finds it useful to remind the child of the picture from the formal training session:

TEACHER: Pushing her is *one* way to get Yvette to sit down. What might happen if you push her?
BENNIE: She might hit me back, but I can't see.
TEACHER: Can you think of a *different* way to get her to sit down?
BENNIE (*angrily*): No!
TEACHER: Do you remember the picture we saw of children at story time and one child wanted another to sit down?
BENNIE: Yeah!
TEACHER: You had lots of ideas that the boy could do. What was one of them?
BENNIE: Please sit down.
YVETTE: (*Sits down.*)
TEACHER: That was a different idea, and Yvette sat down. How do you feel about that?
BENNIE: Happy. (*If such incidents occur before the problem has been presented formally it is still possible to encourage alternative thinking at the child's present level.*)

There are times when a child does not respond to the

dialogue in the style described here, even after the concepts have been taught. The teacher must decide whether to pursue the questioning or to drop it. In one episode Dorothy was hitting Russell because Russell wanted her to share her collage materials. Dorothy, grabbing all the materials, screamed, "You never play with me and now I'm not going to play with you!" The teacher decided not to guide a dialogue for two reasons: Dorothy often does share possessions, and there are times when a child should have the right to play alone; and Dorothy was too emotional to think clearly anyway. In this instance the teacher simply interested Russell in doing something else. More will be said subsequently about using dialogues in emotional situations.

Other incidents of crying or pouting behavior. Sometimes a child is crying and the teacher cannot find out why. In such instances the teacher can involve the children in direct questioning of each other, incorporating into the conversation specific games from the script. For example, if a child is crying the teacher might proceed as follows: "How is Bernard feeling?" *Let the child respond. Offer a choice of happy or sad if necessary:* "Yes, Bernard is sad. He is not happy. How can you tell he is sad?" *If the answer is that he is crying the teacher can say:* "How can you tell he is crying? We can see with our (*point to eyes*) and we can hear with our (*point to ears*)." "How do *you* feel? Do you feel the same way as Bernard or do you feel a different way?" *Let the child respond.* "Would you like to help make Bernard feel happy again?" *If the child says yes he may be encouraged to continue.* "How can you find out why he is so sad? What can you *say* to him to find out why he is so sad?" *Bernard might be brought over and encouraged to play the Do You Like? game (Game 15, Day 19).*

The next dialogue illustrates use of the program style in encouraging a child to think things through before jumping to a quick and faulty conclusion:

TEACHER (*to Linda, who is crying*): Linda, why are you so sad?
LINDA: Richard's chasing me.
TEACHER: Do you know why Richard is chasing you?
LINDA: No.
TEACHER (*brings Richard over*): Linda, how can you find out why Richard's chasing you?

LINDA (*to Richard*) : Why are you chasing me?
RICHARD: I want to play with you.
LINDA: You got nobody to play with?
RICHARD: Nope.
LINDA: OK, I'll play with you.

The result is quite different than if the teacher had said: "Richard, I can't let you chase Linda. Linda doesn't like to be chased." The dialogue allows Linda to learn why she was being chased, which in turn allows her to solve her problem to the satisfaction of both children.

What can a teacher do for a child who is standing by herself in a corner pouting quietly? Debbie was doing just this, and the following conversation took place:

TEACHER: Debbie, are you feeling happy *or* are you feeling sad?
DEBBIE: Sad.
TEACHER: Why are you feeling so sad?
DEBBIE: I want to go to the big room.
TEACHER: Do you remember Allie the Alligator?
DEBBIE: Yeah!
TEACHER: What does Allie like to do?
DEBBIE: Swim.
TEACHER: Does Allie like to swim *all* of the time *or some* of the time?
DEBBIE: Some of the time.
TEACHER: Do you like to be in the big room *all* of the time *or some* of the time?
DEBBIE: All of the time.
TEACHER: How might Allie feel if he swims *all* of the time?
DEBBIE (*smiles*): Tired.
TEACHER: How might you feel if you were in the big room *all* of the time?
DEBBIE: (*Laughs and joins other children in play.*)

This dialogue is another example of directly incorporating concepts from a formal lesson. The child is able to realize at least one reason why it is not feasible to be in the big room all the time. This leaves her feeling more satisfied than if the teacher had simply said, "It's time to be in the classroom now" or even "I know you want to be in the big room now, but it's time to be here now."

A child is failing at something. Another dialogue incorporating concepts beyond alternative thinking from the Allie story was utilized when Gregory was unable to find anyone to play with. After asking several children, each of whom says no, he asks Elizabeth with whom he had played Lotto earlier in the morning:

GREGORY: Elizabeth, let's play Lotto.

ELIZABETH: No, I don't want to.

GREGORY (*very sadly*) : Please.

ELIZABETH (*Continues to shake her head no.*)

GREGORY: Teacher, nobody will play with me.

TEACHER: Gregory, do you want to play with Elizabeth *or* do you want to play Lotto?

GREGORY: I want Elizabeth to play with me.

TEACHER: You and Elizabeth played Lotto today, right?

GREGORY: Right.

TEACHER: Do you think Elizabeth likes to play Lotto *all* of the time or *some* of the time?

GREGORY: Some of the time.

TEACHER: How can you find out what else Elizabeth likes to do?

GREGORY: Ask her.

TEACHER: Go ahead and ask her.

GREGORY (*to Elizabeth*) : Do you like puzzles?

ELIZABETH: Yes.

GREGORY: Will you do a puzzle with me?

ELIZABETH: Yes.

GREGORY: (*Zealously gets out a puzzle and beams.*)

Terry, a child who was not well liked, was just beginning to try solutions other than grabbing, kicking, and hitting. His first attempt at verbal problem-solving was centered around his wanting to join a picnic. After having been rejected when he asked to come in, he brought back some toys and offered, "I have some presents for you." The children continued to ignore him. Terry walked away and started to grab a spinning top from Benjie. The teacher asked Terry if he could think of a different idea. Terry tried, "Can I play with the spinning top?" Benjie said "No!" Because the teacher did not want Terry to experience continued failure with his first attempts at alternative means of problem-solving, she did not continue with the usual dialogue (for example, "Oh, he said no. Can you think of a different idea?"). The following dialogue begins with Benjie just having said no to Terry's request for the spinning top:

TEACHER: Benjie, why won't you let Terry play with the spinning top?

BENJIE: 'Cause he never gives it back.

TEACHER: Terry, what can you say to Benjie so he'll know you'll give it back?

TERRY: I'll give it back.

TEACHER: Oh, Benjie, can you give Terry a chance? He said he'd give it back.

BENJIE: No, he never gives it back.

The teacher, not wanting Terry to experience failure but at the same time wanting to avoid forcing Benjie to give in, continues:

TEACHER: I'll stay right here and I'll make sure he gives it back. It would make him feel very happy if you gave him a chance.

BENJIE: OK. (*To Terry:*) But you can only have two turns. (*Terry spins the top two times and gives it back to Benjie. The teacher praises them both. Terry is feeling very good. About ten minutes later Terry again asks Benjie for the top. Benjie says, "No, you won't give it back." Terry, dejected, starts to walk away. The teacher again talks to Benjie.*)

TEACHER: Benjie, did Terry give it back to you before?

BENJIE: Yeah, but he won't now.

TEACHER: How can you find out if he'll give it back?

BENJIE: (*to Terry*) : Will you give it back?

TERRY: Yeah.

BENJIE: OK, you can have five turns. (*The teacher again praises both children, and Benjie and Terry continue taking turns for about five minutes longer.*)

This example illustrates how a teacher sometimes uses a dialogue in the style of the program to guide a youngster toward a successful outcome to his problem. Nevertheless the teacher is not telling the child what to say or think: she is merely manipulating the circumstances temporarily to give Terry a feeling of success.

How can a teacher handle difficult situations before prerequisite concepts have been learned in the formal training? Experience suggests that the general dialogue techniques can be used but that the child who is having a problem should not be told what to say or be given specific solutions to that problem. If the child cannot identify emotions before they come up formally, that line of questioning can be dropped and emphasis placed on alternative ideas, even though he is able to think of more ideas as the formal training program progresses.

Avoiding Potential Problems

Certain situations occur frequently in group settings with young children. When children run inside and someone might get hurt, one of three statements is generally made to the child: "Don't run"; "Walk!"; or "If you run you might fall and hurt yourself."

Consistent with the style of the program, the following dialogue is typical when children run inside:

TEACHER: Johnny, is running inside a good idea?
JOHNNY (*stops and smiles*): No.
TEACHER: What might happen if you run inside?
JOHNNY: I might fall.
TEACHER: How might you feel if you fall?
JOHNNY: Sad.
TEACHER: Can you think of another idea?
JOHNNY: Walk.

It is simply a matter of letting the child think about the potential consequences of running inside. He does not need to be told to walk. Furthermore when he tells the teacher, he is more likely to walk then to continue running.

One morning Eddie had his hand in the egg-beater when the children were mixing soapflakes and water. The teacher asked, "Is that a good place for your hand?" Eddie, adopting the program style himself, replied, "No, because I might get hurt," whereupon he took hold of the handle. The teacher did not need to tell him to take his hand out of the beater.

In Game 17 the children are shown a picture of a girl falling off her bike. When asked why she might have fallen off, most children respond with "She was riding too fast." When Nancy was riding too fast the teacher reminded her of the bike problem:

TEACHER: What might happen if you ride that bike so fast?
NANCY: I might fall off.

TEACHER: Do you remember the little girl in the picture who fell off the bike?

NANCY: Yeah, 'cause she was riding too fast.

TEACHER: Can you think of a different way to ride that bike?

NANCY: Yeah! (*Rides off more slowly.*)

Another episode illustrates the use of the program style when the children are distracted from an activity and place themselves in a dangerous situation. Eight children were attracted to a conversation between a visitor and a child. They came over to the table where that conversation was taking place and stood with their pencil points precariously close to each other. In the style of the training program the teacher approached the group: "Are your pencils in a good place when you're standing so close to each other?" The children looked at their pencils, laughed, and said no. "Can anyone think of a *different* place for your pencils?" One child placed his pencil behind his ear and gleefully shouted, "Now I won't poke him!", pointing to the closest boy. The children cheerfully followed suit, and no more needed to be said.

This style can be used whenever a child does something that might lead to harm or discomfort. Unless the child has to be physically stopped because danger is imminent, he should be guided in thinking the situation through just as in handling problem behavior. An important element in many of these situations is the help the teacher offers the child in focusing on the presence of a danger through its consequences. The same applies whenever the child refuses or forgets to do something that would benefit him:

TEACHER: Alice, is it a good idea to paint at the easel without an apron?

ALICE: (*No answer.*)

TEACHER: What might happen if you paint without an apron?

ALICE: My dress will get dirty.

TEACHER: Can you think of a way so you won't get dirty?

ALICE: Put on an apron.

Sometimes the dialogue style of the program avoids problems and thus enhances a feeling of warmth between the teacher and the child. This result is exemplified by the following two episodes.

Johnny came to school and said, "See my new shoes." His teacher responded, "How do they make you feel?" "Mad," replied

Johnny. "Why do they make you feel mad?" "Because," said Johnny, "they hurt."

From this conversation we learn several points of interest. When children come in and say something similar to "See my new shoes," the typical response of the teacher is: "They're very nice." End of conversation. In the present case, using the language of the training program allowed the child to express himself and to feel that someone cared how he felt. It also afforded the teacher an opportunity to learn that not only did the child understand the concept *mad* but that, contrary to her expectation, his shoes did not please him.

In another episode Linwood had tied a rope to the door in the playground that leads to the inside of the building and was pulling the rope. A teacher aide from another classroom who was not familiar with the language of the training program said, "Linwood, you can't tie that rope to the door. People can't get in." When the aide walked away the training teacher came over and said, "Whose good idea was that to tie the rope to this door?" Linwood said, "Mine!" The teacher then added, "Very good idea, Linwood. Now can you think of a different good place to tie the rope?" Linwood took the rope off the door, tied it to the fence, and said, "I tied it to the fence." Then he began pulling and swinging on it again. The teacher smiled and said, "Very good, you thought of a different good place to tie the rope and now people can get in the door."

This episode employed the strategy of guiding the child to alternative means to satisfy his goal of pulling the rope. The child responded positively to the teacher's understanding that his goal was to pull the rope and not to prevent people from getting in the door. Employing a negative "you can't" too often decreases self-esteem and brings on the feeling of not being understood. Our program highlights the fact that, in addition, "you can't" does not afford the child the opportunity to think of alternative ways to satisfy his goal without negative consequences.

Application in Informal Situations

It is useful to review the concepts taught formally when the children are together informally and relatively calm, such as at juice or lunch time. Informal dialogues can be employed after each formal lesson, beginning with the first day. The children like these reviews; they enjoy using what they have learned.

After the first lesson focusing on the word *is*, it is useful for the teacher to begin a conversation such as: "Is Johnny a boy?" *Let the children respond.* "Yes, Johnny *is* a boy. Is Mary a girl?" *Let the children respond.* "Yes, Mary *is* a girl."

The teacher can then switch to: "Is this juice?" *Let the children respond.* "Yes, this *is* juice. Is this a cracker?" *Let the children respond.* "Yes, this *is* a cracker."

After the second day the teacher can focus on the words *a* and *some*. "Is Johnny *a* boy or is Johnny *some* boys?" *Let the group reply.* "Are Mary and Rochelle *a* girl or are they *some* girls?" *Let the group reply.*

Following the games that teach the word *not*, the teacher can pick up an object such as a cracker and say: "This is a cracker. This is *not* a———. This is *not* a———. This is juice. This is *not* ———."

One way to combine the words *not* and *same-different* and the Do You Like? game is for the teacher to ask each child at the table if he likes dogs. "Johnny and Jimmy like dogs. Peter and Sandra do *not* like dogs. Do Johnny and Peter like the *same* thing?" *Let the children respond.* "No, they like———things. Is it all right for *different* children to like *different* things?" *Let the group reply.* "How can we find out what Peter and Sandra like?" *Let the group respond.* "Johnny, it's your turn to find out what Peter likes." If Johnny has not caught on to the game the teacher can help him by saying: "Peter, do you like———?" Then Johnny may be encouraged to continue.

Children also enjoy playing the I Am Not game. The teacher can start by saying: "I am not a balloon. Jimmy, you are not a———." The game can be played exactly like Game 3 in the formal script. If one child simply repeats what another has said, the teacher can ask: "Can you think of something different that you're not? You're not a———."

It is also easy to use the word *and*. "I am holding a cracker *and* a cup of milk. Now I am not holding a cracker." The children can be encouraged to tell what they are and are not holding. The teacher can also ask: "Who *is* at our table?" *Let the group reply.* "Who is *not* at our table?" *Let the group reply.* Yes, Peter *is* at our table. Robbie is *not* at our table. Peter and Robbie are at *different* tables."

The word *different* can be used in other ways as well. The teacher can pick up a cracker and a glass of juice. "This is a cracker. This is juice. Is a cracker the *same* as juice?" *Let the group reply.* "No, they are————." The children enjoy shouting out the word *different* once the words *same* and *different* have been taught in the formal lesson.

The words *happy* and *sad* can be incorporated in similar ways. "Who is feeling happy?" *Let the group respond.* "Who is not feeling sad?" *Let the group respond.* "Who is not feeling happy?" *Let the group respond.*

The prerequisite and pre-problem-solving concepts can be used in other situations. If a child in the classroom is crying the teacher might ask the closest child to her: "How does ———— feel?" *Let the group respond.* "Yes, she feels sad. How can you tell she feels sad?" *The children will probably say that she is crying. Ask:* "How can you tell she is crying?" *If the children say "she has tears,"* *follow with:* "How can you tell she has tears? We can see with our (*point to eyes*) *and* we can hear with our (*point to ears*). What can we do to make ———— feel happy again?" *After the children respond, follow with:* "That's one way." *The crying child can be brought within earshot and the children can be encouraged to make the sad child happy again.*

Another useful technique in guiding children to become aware of each other during free-play periods is to approach a child standing alone and ask: "Randolph, what is Bobby doing? *Give a choice if necessary.* "Yes, Bobby is doing a puzzle. How can you tell? You can see with your (*point to eyes*). Does Bobby do puzzles *all* of the time or *some* of the time?" *Let the child respond.* "Yes, *some* of the time. Bobby does different things at different times. Randolph, what do you like to do?" *If there is no answer:* "Do you like to paint?" *If he answers yes:* "Do you like to paint *all* of the time or *some* of the time?" *Let the child respond.* "Yes, you like to do different things at different times."

As in Game 15 of the formal script children can be asked

what they like to do and what they do *not* like to do, and differences can be pointed out: "Johnny does like to paint. Sally does *not* like to paint. Johnny and Sally like *different* things. Is it OK for different children to like different things?"

The script style can also be applied in group situations outside the formal training, such as at music or story time. At music time it is possible to play games similar to the one with trinkets during formal training, substituting musical instruments for trinkets.

"Robert, what instrument do you have?" *Let Robert reply.* "James, what instrument do you have?" *Let James reply. To the group:* "Do Robert and James have the *same* instrument? No, they have ———— ones." *Each child may be asked.*

"Robert, do you want to play the instrument that you have or would you rather play one that someone else has?" *If Robert says he would like the one Debbie has, the teacher may say:* "Robert, can you think of a way to get Debbie to let you have her drum?" *Let Robert respond. If Debbie says no to Robert the teacher asks:* "Robert, can you think of a different idea?" *If Debbie continues to say no Robert can be asked if he would like to keep his instrument or if he can think of a way to get someone else to let him have his instrument.* Each child may have a turn until everyone ends up with the instrument he wants. If there is grabbing, the dialogues used for hurting or grabbing may be applied.

The general vocabulary in the script can be used when reading any story to a child or a group. For example, two objects pictured on a page can be used to ask: "Is ———— the *same* as ———— or are they *different?* Is the boy doing the *same* thing as this boy or are they doing something *different?*" The children can be asked what a boy in the story is not doing, how he is feeling or not feeling. If someone in the story is depicted as being sad the children can be asked what another character in the story can do to help the sad person feel happy again.

Any time the children are together the vocabulary can be implemented. One day when the children all had crayons and paper, the teacher asked if everyone was doing the same thing. One girl brought over some blocks and shouted, "I'm going to do something *different!*"

Quite often in a classroom a number of children all talk at

once when asked a question. Sometimes this is perfectly acceptable, but when one particular child is called on the teacher probably does not want every child to shout out at once. Emphasizing the words *all, same,* and *different,* one teacher used the following dialogue.

"If *all* of you shout at the *same* time, can I hear (*pointing to ears*) what Darren is saying?" *Let the children respond.* "If I want to hear what Darren is saying is it a good idea if you *all* talk at the *same* time or at *different* times?" *Let the children respond.* "I'm going to ask Darren the question again. Are you *all* going to answer or just Darren?" *Let the children respond.* "Good, just Darren." After Darren was called on the teacher followed with: "Now I'm going to ask Rochelle a question." In game form the children enjoyed not talking until each heard his own name.

Any game in the script can be utilized in these ways. The important point is to allow the child to do the talking even though it is more difficult at times to encourage the child to explain why and what might happen next than it is to tell him.

6

General Use of Program Principles and Techniques

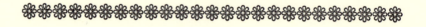

Experience with both formal and informal use of the script has functioned as a springboard to a more general dialogue format that the teacher can use to handle the wide range of problem situations that occur. This general format and the formal training script share in common the same operating principles and goals.

Consistent throughout is the basic principle of guiding the child to think without telling him what to think. Whether or not the child responds, the teacher should avoid telling the child what to do. Helping guide a child to think rather than solving his problem for him requires a change in orientation for most adults. We are used to telling children what we believe and even what they should believe and feel. The focus is generally on getting the "right" answer into the child in a direct way. The focus of our program is on stimulating and encouraging the child's own thought processes. The adult may need to teach certain basic language concepts, but after that he functions as a guide to the social problem-solving of the child. The specific techniques through which this goal is achieved are enumerated in this chapter. The types of situation are the same as those used when presenting dialogues that actually occurred.

Before we spell out specific dialogue techniques, the prerequisite word-concepts should be listed. It is crucial for the teacher to have these word-concepts in mind. Experience indicates that once they have been incorporated the dialogues flow smoothly. These prerequisite word-concepts are: *is-is not, all-some, all* of the time-*some* of the time, *and, same-different, might-maybe, happy-sad-mad, why-because.* Using these word-concepts as basic ingredients the teacher can apply the following techniques in guiding the child through typical problem situations. With each illustrated technique is its cognitive goal.

Interpersonal Conflict

Child Initiates Hurting or Grabbing. Rather than telling the child who hits and grabs that such behavior is not allowed, or even suggesting to him a more positive alternative, the present approach guides him to think about what he is doing.

TEACHER: Johnny, why did you hit (grab from) Peter?

Causal thinking: the child is guided to think about his act in light of his motives.

CHILD: ———.

TEACHER: Hitting (grabbing) is one thing you can do. Is that a good idea?

Consequential thinking: the child is oriented to evaluate his act.

CHILD: ———.

TEACHER (*if the child does not refer to emotions*): How might hitting (grabbing from) Peter make Peter feel?

Awareness of emotions: the child is guided to appreciate the emotional impact of his act on others.

CHILD: ———. (*If the child does not respond, the choice of happy or sad or mad can be offered, to which children usually respond.*)

TEACHER: Yes, he might feel sad (mad). What else might happen if you hit (grab from) Peter?

Alternative consequences: the child is guided to think of more than one potential consequence.

CHILD: ———.

TEACHER: That might happen. Hitting is *one* way to ———. (*Repeat the child's reason for hitting or grabbing.*) Can you think of a *different* idea?

Alternative solutions: the child is guided to think of a different course of action.

CHILD: ———.

TEACHER (*if the child does not respond*): Can you think of something you can say to make him feel happy again?

Solution and consequential thinking: the child is encouraged to find an alternative course of action in light of another's feelings.

CHILD: ———.

TEACHER: That's an idea. Go ahead and try it.

The child is encouraged to translate thought into action.

TEACHER (*if the child's idea is successful*): Very good, you thought of that all by yourself. How does that make you feel?

Consequential thinking: the child is encouraged to act in light of his own feelings.

TEACHER (*if the child's idea is unsuccessful*): Oh, that idea did not work (make him happy). Can you think of a different idea?

The child is encouraged to think of alternative solutions when action based on one idea is unsuccessful.

Child Reciprocates Hurting or Grabbing.   Quite frequently a child reciprocates because "he hit me first" or "my mommy told me to hit back." The teacher accepts his feelings and proceeds with a dialogue similar to the preceding one:

TEACHER: Yes, he hit you first (your mommy did tell you to hit back). Hitting (grabbing) is *one* thing you can do. How did it make you feel when Robert hit (grabbed from) you?

Consequential thinking: the child is guided to think about his own reaction to being hit or having something grabbed from him.

CHILD: ———. (*If the child does not respond, the choice of happy or sad or mad can be given.*)

TEACHER: Yes, you felt mad (sad). How do you think Robert feels when you hit (grab from) him?

Consequential thinking: the child is guided to evaluate the effect of his act on another.

CHILD: ———.

TEACHER: He might feel mad (sad). Robert, you feel mad. Robin, you feel mad. Can one of you think of a way to feel happy?

Solutions: the child is guided to think of solutions in light of unpleasant emotions.

CHILD: ———.

TEACHER: That's one thing you could try. Is that a good idea?

Consequential thinking: the child is guided to evaluate his own ideas.

CHILD: ———.

TEACHER (*to the child who responds*): Can you find out if (the other child) likes that idea? (*Encourage him to ask.*)

The child is guided to find out how others feel and to appreciate that different children might be made happy by different things.

TEACHER (*if the other child says yes*): Oh, that would make him happy. Go ahead and try it.

The child is encouraged to try out his own idea.

TEACHER (*if the other child says no*): Oh, that would not make him happy. Can you think of a *different* idea?

Alternative solutions: the child is encouraged to think of another solution when one does not work.

If both children are too emotional to respond, a third child can be brought over and asked for an idea to make Robert and Robin feel happy. Several children can be brought over and encouraged to offer ideas and try them out.

Child Cries or Pouts. Two general techniques are helpful when a child is crying or being sullen for no apparent reason: using the program style directly with the child, and bringing other children into the conversation. If the child is open to responding, the teacher can incorporate the following dialogue into a conversation:

TEACHER: I can see that you are crying (pouting). Can you tell me how you feel?

The child is guided to think about his feelings.

CHILD: ———.
TEACHER: Can you tell me why you feel sad?

Causal thinking.

CHILD: ———.

TEACHER (*whether the child answers or not*): Can you tell me something that would make you feel happy again?

The child is guided to think about his feelings and what he wants.

If the child replies that he wants something which is feasible, the teacher can simply satisfy his desire. If the child is sad because Billy won't play with him, the following approach is useful:

TEACHER: Can you think of something to do so Billy will play with you?

The child is guided to think of a solution to his problem.

CHILD: ———.

TEACHER: Can you find out if Billy likes that idea?

The child is guided to appreciate that different children might like to do different things and that he must find out.

CHILD: ———.

TEACHER (*if successful*): Good, you thought of that all by yourself. How does that make you feel?

The child is made aware of his own feelings.

TEACHER (*if unsuccessful*): Oh, you'll have to think of a different idea.

Alternative solutions.

If the child is sad because the teacher is unable to satisfy a request, the following approach is useful. Suppose the child wants to go outside:

TEACHER (*accepting the child's feelings*): I know you feel sad because I can't let you go outside now. Can you tell me why I can't let you go outside now?

The child is encouraged to think about the consequences of going outside when everyone else is inside.

CHILD: ———.

TEACHER (*if the child does not respond*): What might happen if you go outside and all of us are inside?

Consequential thinking.

CHILD: ————.

TEACHER: Can you think of something you can do inside?

The child is guided to discover for himself what he can do to feel better.

Another dialogue that can be used when the child makes a request that cannot be granted follows the puppet story about Allie. The dialogue described in Chapter Five is an example. If the child is too upset or unwilling to respond, other children can be brought into the situation. If, for example, Sally is crying, Chris can be brought over.

TEACHER: Chris, how does Sally feel?

The child is guided to think about the feelings of another child.

CHRIS: ————.

TEACHER: Yes, she's sad. How can you tell she's sad? You can see with your *(point to eyes) and* you can hear with your *(point to ears)*:

Alternative thinking and sensitivity to others' feelings: the child is guided to recognize that there is more than one way to find out how another child feels.

TEACHER: Does Sally feel sad *all* of the time or *some* of the time?

The child is guided to recognize that the same child can feel different ways at different times.

CHRIS: ————.

TEACHER: Yes, Sally feels sad some of the time. Chris *(within earshot of Sally)*, can you think of a way to make Sally feel happy again?

Alternative solutions: the child is guided to think of ways to help another child feel better.

CHRIS: ————.

TEACHER: That's one idea. How can you find out if Sally likes that idea?

The child is helped to appreciate that different children might like different things.

CHRIS: ———.

TEACHER (*if successful*): Good, you thought of that all by yourself. How does that make you feel?

The child thinks about his own feelings.

TEACHER (*if unsuccessful*): Oh, you'll have to think of a different idea.

Alternative solutions.

   If children are gathered around, the teacher can ask each child how to help make Sally feel happy. The children can be encouraged to begin with "Do you like ———?", following the style of the Do You Like? game (Game 15 in the formal script).
   Often a child cries or pouts for an obvious reason. When one child attacks or belittles another and the attacked child responds by crying rather than by hitting back, the teacher can talk to both children. If Randy is crying because Kenneth hit him the following dialogue can take place:

TEACHER: Randy, why are you so sad?

Causal thinking.

CHILD: ———.

TEACHER (*within earshot of Randy*): Kenneth, how does your hitting Randy make him feel?

Consequential thinking: the child is guided to think about his act in light of its consequences for another child's emotions.

CHILD: ———. (*If Kenneth does not answer, the choice of happy or sad or mad can be given.*)

TEACHER: Yes, he feels sad. What might happen next if you hit Randy? (*If needed:* "What might Randy do or say if you hit him?")

Consequential thinking: the child evaluates his act in light of the other child's reaction.

CHILD: ———.

TEACHER: That's one thing that might happen. Can you think of something you can do or say so Randy will not ———? (*Repeat the consequence given by the child.*)

Solutions: the child is guided to think of what alternative behavior might produce a different consequence.

CHILD: ———.

TEACHER: That's one idea. Can you find out if Randy likes that idea?

Sensitivity to preferences of others is encouraged.

If Kenneth is too emotional to respond, other children can be brought over and asked what can be done to help make Randy feel happy again.

Child Is Failing At Something. Not uncommon is the child who whines, "Johnny won't play with me" or "Johnny won't let me ———." Often he is unhappy because he does not make the distinction between another child not wanting to play with him and the other child not wanting to do what he wants to do. A typical dialogue for such a situation follows. The dialogue includes three concepts that are given special emphasis throughout the program: some of the time versus all of the time; asking to find things out about people; the Do You Like? game.

TEACHER: Carrie, what do you want Robert to do?

The child classifies in his own mind what he wants (his problem).

CARRIE: Build a tower.

TEACHER: Do you want to play with Robert *or* do you want to build a tower?

The child thinks further about what he really wants.

CARRIE: Play with Robert.

TEACHER: Do you think Robert likes to build a tower *all* of the time or *some* of the time?

The child is guided toward realizing that the same child likes to do different things at different times.

CARRIE: ———.

TEACHER: How can you find out if Robert wants to build a tower now?

The child is helped to find out what another child wants and to appreciate that another child might not want do the same thing he does.

CARRIE: ———. (*If the child says "ask," encourage him to follow through.*)

TEACHER (*when Robert says no*): Oh, Robert, does *not* want to build a tower now. Can you think of something different to ask him to do? (*The child can be encouraged to use the Do You Like? game.*)

Alternative solutions.

CARRIE: ———.

TEACHER (*if successful*): Oh, Robert does want to play with you. Robert just did not want to build a tower.

There is reassurance, clarification that Robert did want to play with Carrie, and reinforcement for finding out behavior.

An unusual but simple situation is when a child complains that another child will not let him play with something: "He won't let me have any clay!" The following guidance is usually effective:

TEACHER (*to both children*): What can we do when two children want to play with the *same* thing at the *same* time?

Solutions: the children are encouraged to find their own solutions to the problem.

If sharing or some form of playing together is not offered, the teacher can ask the first child if he can think of something to say to the second child. If the child is just beginning to use "ask" as a solution, it is important to help the child avoid failure. The teacher can ask the second child why he will not let the first child have any clay. If it is unreasonable to share, the teacher can explain: "There really is not enough clay for two children to play at the *same* time. Can you think of something *different* to do for a little while?"

Avoiding Potential Problems

Besides the incidents of potential danger or discomfort that actually took place, the style of the training program can be used in any similar situation. Typical incidents include a child standing in front of a moving swing, climbing incorrectly on gym equipment, or using tools incorrectly. The same dialogue can apply in all such situations:

TEACHER: Is ——— a good idea?

Consequential thinking: the child is guided to evaluate his act.

CHILD: ———.

TEACHER: How might you feel if you (fall, hurt yourself, and so on)?

Consequential thinking: the child is guided to evaluate his act in light of its consequences for his own feelings.

CHILD: ———.

TEACHER: Can you think of a different (place to stand, way to climb, way to hammer)?

Alternative solutions: the child is guided to redirect his own behavior.

Sometimes a child is damaging property, such as drawing on a table or cutting something with scissors that he should not be cutting. A useful dialogue is:

TEACHER: Is painting on the wall a good idea?

Consequential thinking: the child evaluates his act.

CHILD: ————.

TEACHER: Why is painting on the wall not a good idea?

Consequential and causal thinking: the child is guided to think about the effect of his act.

CHILD: ————.

TEACHER: Can you think of a different place to paint?

Alternative thinking: the child is guided to redirect his behavior.

If the child says yes to the question "Is that a good idea?", the teacher can follow with: "Why is that a good idea? How do you think that makes me feel? Can you think of a place to paint that will not make me feel angry?" When the adult must intervene because property is being damaged, the goal is for the child to recognize how an adult might feel about it and to develop solutions to avoid such problems in the future. But it is important to recognize that the child's motive may not be to damage property. This may only be a by-product of a desire to paint or create something. In such a case the teacher can provide paper and ask the child if he can think of a different place to paint.

Further Comments on Technique

Dialogues are effective after word-concepts and pre-problem-solving skills have been taught. Although some youngsters are familiar with the words *and, or,* and *not,* teaching them within the context of interpersonal situations sets the stage for their role in problem-solving. The words *same-different, some-all, might-maybe,* and those that designate feeling—*happy, sad, mad*—are unfamiliar to many youngsters before training. Though many teachers teach these concepts in their curriculum, their sequence in this program and their use in dialogues have the specific goal of helping the child develop a problem-solving style that will mediate behavioral adjustment.

The key questions and phrases that permeate the dialogues have more meaning for the child after certain basic games have been experienced. One key question, "Does Johnny like to play with blocks all of the time or some of the time?", is used to help a child understand why Johnny might not want to play with blocks at a given moment. The phrase can also be used to help a nagging child understand why he cannot have something he wants immediately. However, the real implications behind this line of questioning become meaningful only after the "Allie the Alligator" puppet stories have been presented. The children appreciate and understand how Allie the Alligator loves to swim, but not all the time.

Another key question, "How can you find out?" about another's feelings, preferences, or desires, has more meaning after the seeing, hearing, and Do You Like? games have been introduced. Finding out how another child feels or thinks about his own feelings has more meaning after the games on emotions become familiar.

As mentioned, an effective technique for eliciting a response from a nonresponding child is to ask a question and then offer him a simple choice. The two most frequent concepts involved in such choices are *same-different* and *happy-sad*. In addition to knowing the words involved the child must be able to respond to the concept *or*, taught in the earliest games. Two important guiding questions, "What might happen next?" and "Can you think of a different idea?", are predicated on the child's knowledge of the words *might* and *different*.

Any dialogue can of course be used at any time. Though the questions will probably be meaningful to more children after the formal lessons, their constant repetition helps guide each child to develop a problem-solving style.

Often a dialogue with a child is aided by bringing a third party into the situation. When two children are engaged in a conflict situation emotions are sometimes too intense for either child to respond to dialogue. It is often possible to bring a third child over and ask him what he can think of to make the children feel better. Sometimes children respond to another child more readily than to the teacher.

At other times the teacher may have to take direct action to soothe the hurt feelings of one child by consoling him or reduce the anxiety of another child by protecting him from the domination of an aggressor. As soon as the feeling or tension has been reduced, however, appropriate dialogue ought to be pursued, especially about how each child feels and what can be done to change the feelings.

When a solution is offered and accepted by two children in a conflict situation, or offered by a child about to engage in an activity of potential danger, the teacher should encourage the child to carry out that solution. If a child offers "ask" as a solution to obtain a toy from another child, the teacher should encourage him to go ahead and ask. If a child offers "walk" when he is asked about running inside, the teacher should follow with: "You thought of that all by yourself. Can you go ahead and do that?"

Besides carrying through a solution, follow-through also becomes important whenever promise is made between one child and another that ends with the usual "I'll give it right back." The teacher should watch the situation and encourage the child to be sure to give it back. When a child cannot have something he wants and is able to think of something different to do, the teacher should notice whether the child does become occupied in that activity and comment on it.

The point of emphasizing the need for follow-through is to help guard against starting a dialogue and then leaving before the episode has been completed. Although young children are usually responsive to the guidance given by the dialogues, initially most are not able to carry them through on their own.

Sometimes the dialogues are not effective and their use is better postponed. Sometimes a crying child just needs to cry or an angry child just needs time to be angry. There are also times when a child is so emotional that it would be impossible for him to respond to a dialogue, at least for quite a while. One little girl, JoAnn, jumped on a bike that the teacher told Larry he could ride. JoAnn would not get off, and when Larry hit her she became more stubborn. When it became clear that guiding a dialogue would only reach deaf ears, the teacher had to take a different approach: "JoAnn, I cannot let you ride the bike now. Would you like to sit on the step here *or* would you like to sit on my lap for a little while until you feel better?" JoAnn, needing such support, chose to sit on the teacher's lap. The teacher reminded Larry that JoAnn was waiting for the bike and that he could ride around a few more times. This follow-through gave JoAnn both comfort and a sense of trust. The teacher urged Larry to give JoAnn the bike himself, which he did. Here the teacher wished to avoid hurting anyone's self-esteem.

JoAnn was not ordered off the bike but was given comfort when she needed it. Larry was not told that his turn was up but was given advance notice and allowed to give JoAnn the bike himself. In most problem situations, however, the dialogues can be used and the children feel good about thinking of their own solutions, which they usually carry out.

Our program carries one step further the present-day techniques used by trained teachers of preschool children. If a teacher is inclined to use the positive approach of telling the child what to do rather than what not to do (see Read, 1955), our program asserts that through carefully guided dialogues the child can learn to think and decide for himself what and what not to do.

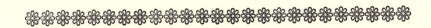

7

Research
Evaluation

In developing our program a great deal of attention was given to careful research to ensure that the program could do what it was intended to do—alter thinking and behavior in a predictable way. It is one thing to design and develop a seemingly reasonable program on the basis of correlational research and quite another to demonstrate with hard data that applying the program does produce such change. To ensure correct interpretation of the program's impact on thinking and behavior, three evaluation studies were conducted while the program was operating in Get Set (Head Start) centers in Philadelphia. The first two studies were preliminary; the third was a final, comprehensive, and sophisticated evaluation of the program.

First Preliminary Evaluation

The design in this study (Shure, Spivack, and Gordon, 1972) included three groups, one training and two controls, from two inner-city Get Set centers. The training group consisted of twenty-two children drawn from five classes and divided into four small groups. The first control, the Attention group, consisted of eleven children divided into two small groups. The second control, the no-treatment group, consisted of the twenty-one remaining children from the two participating centers. Prior to training, all three groups were equivalent on all measures used to assess change in thinking and behavior.

The training groups were led by research assistants (college students) trained in working with the script. The children were taken out of their classrooms for fifty mornings over a ten-week period. Early sessions ran for about five minutes, building to a maximum of twenty minutes after five weeks. The sessions were held with each of the four training groups in the mornings, leaving the remainder of the day uninterrupted. The same pattern was followed with the two attention groups, who during their sessions engaged in animal imitations, ball-rolling, finger games, singing, and story-telling—activities which, like those of the training group, stimulated leader-child interaction. The no-treatment group received neither training nor special attention outside of the regular activities of the centers. Because the teachers would be rating behavior before and after the training, they knew no details of either the training or the attention activities. Nor did they know that the objective of the program was to enhance behavioral adjustment. They were told and completely accepted that the purpose of the program was to help children think about interpersonal problem-solving.

Regarding changes in problem-solving ability (measured by the PIPS test), all twenty-two trained children increased their ability to give relevant solutions to real-life problems. An increase occurred in only four of the eleven children in the attention group and eleven of the twenty-one in the no-treatment group. The greater number of trained children who improved when compared to the two control groups was statistically significant ($\chi^2 = 24.78$, $p < 0.001$). In a similar fashion the trained children increased in the total number of different solution categories they could think of, and fewer of them gave irrelevant responses after training. As was true of the total number of relevant solutions given, both these findings significantly differentiated the training group from the two control groups. These improvements in thinking were unrelated to measured intelligence, indicating that the program enhanced specific interpersonal thinking skills distinct from general intelligence.

Overt behavioral adjustment was measured with well-standardized and reliable rating scales. The teachers rated each child before and after the intervention program. Though not statistically significant, 50 percent of the children who were trained increased their ability to delay gratification compared with 18 and 26 percent of the attention and no-treatment control groups. Within the training group, however, seven of the eight children originally classified as behaviorally aberrant showed improvement in delay ability in contrast to only three of ten in the control groups ($CR = 2.00, p < 0.05$). Children showing the most behavioral improvement also showed the greatest gain in the trained problem-solving skills, indicating that it was the improved thinking that brought about the improved overt behavioral adjustment.

On similar behavioral scales measuring each child's comprehension and general alertness in the classroom, active involvement in activities, and positive relationship with the teacher, the children receiving training showed more positive change than the control children. A well-standardized classroom adjustment scale consisting of eleven behavioral factors revealed that trained children who improved most in problem-solving skills also improved in seven of eleven factors, a statistically significant change when compared with the remainder of the trained children. Again a direct link between improved thinking (through training) and improved behavioral adjustment was established.

In summary this preliminary study provided strong evidence that the script, administered by research assistants with no teaching experience, leads to enhanced capacity to think in terms of solutions to typical interpersonal problems and that this enhanced capacity leads to improved behavioral adjustment outside the training.

The Second Preliminary Evaluation

A second preliminary evaluation of the program (Shure and Spivack, 1972a) was carried out with a larger sample of children to determine whether the program would be effective if administered by the Get Set teachers themselves (rather than research assistants) and to explore in greater depth the thinking skills being enhanced.

Fifty-two Get Set preschool children were trained, and forty-two matched children served as controls. The untrained children merely received the usual Get Set program because the first study indicated that the positive effects of the program were not due to the added attention received during training. Four Get Set teachers were trained to apply the script during weekly two-hour meetings while the program was in progress. During these meetings the script for that week was reviewed, specific lessons were dramatized, questions were answered about technique, and suggestions for detailed script improvements were discussed with the teachers. Each trained teacher divided her class into two small groups of about seven children each for twenty minutes of daily training; the control teachers divided their classes in a similar fashion each day for story time.

The results of having teachers apply the program closely paralleled the prior results using research assistants as agents of change. The trained children improved significantly in ability to conceptualize solutions to everyday problems, ability to conceptualize cause and effects in human behavior, and sensitivity to consequences of interpersonal acts. The children were classified as adjusted or aberrant (acting out or inhibited) on the basis of detailed, reliable behavioral ratings of teachers before and after the training period. The percentage of trained children classified as adjusted after training (85 percent) was significantly greater than that before training (52 percent) (CR = 3.40, $p < 0.01$). Sixty percent of the control group were classified as adjusted before the program, and about the same percentage (57 percent) were so classified afterward. Again, and most importantly, those children in the training group who exhibited the greatest increase in problem-solving ability also showed the most positive behavioral change.

Beyond repeating the findings of the earlier study, the results of the second study also indicated that nursery school teachers working in Get Set centers could be trained to use it as part of their overall day-care program. Their reaction to the program was consistently positive. This second study also indicated that those children most in need of training (those with the lowest problem-solving scores before training) would get the most out of the program. Although both adjusted and behaviorally aberrant trained children improved significantly in their thinking, an adjusted correlation between initial scores and gain scores was -0.38 ($N = 52$, $p < 0.01$), indicating that those starting with relatively low scores gained significantly more than those starting with relatively high scores. The insignificant $+0.07$ correlation for the untrained group of children was further evidence of the effect of the training program.

Third Program Evaluation

On September 1, 1971, a grant was received from the Applied Research Branch, National Institute of Mental Health, Dept. of Health, Education, and Welfare to conduct a long-range, thorough evaluation of the program. This grant afforded an opportunity to confirm previous findings with larger numbers of children and to refine means of measuring program effectiveness (see Shure and Spivack, 1973).

Twenty Get Set classes from nine schools in inner-city Philadelphia took part in this evaluation. A hundred and thirteen children from ten classes were trained, and 106 children from ten classes served as controls. The training and control classes were equated on all measures beforehand.

Before training, all children in both training and control classes were rated by their teachers to assess their level and type of behavioral adjustment in the classroom. As in previous studies a child was finally classified as impulsive (impatient, nagging, grabby, easily upset with low frustration tolerance), inhibited (exhibiting abnormal control of feelings and behavior), or behaviorally adjusted (neither impulsive nor inhibited). Four new behavioral measures were added because preliminary data indicated that they too correlated with the cognitive measures of problem-solving ability. The first new measure yielded the degree to which each child showed concern for others and offered help to other children in distress. The second measured the extent to which the child was liked by his classmates in that they sought him out and enjoyed being with him. The third measured the degree to which the child showed initiative, and the fourth measured the degree to which the child completed activities and overcame obstacles by himself (that is, was autonomous in his functioning).

Interpersonal problem-solving ability was measured in essentially the same ways as in preliminary studies. The PIPS test was used to measure alternative thinking capacity. Stories similar to those used previously provided a measure of each child's readiness to see the causes of human events. The earlier measure of consequential thinking was revised to make it more sensitive to individual differences; essentially it tapped the child's capacity to conceptualize alternative consequences to acts.

The program ran for twelve weeks; the teachers were trained in its use at weekly three-hour meetings. The teachers knew nothing about the cognitive measures used before and after the program to assess its effectiveness. They were told that the purpose of the program was to enhance each child's problem-solving language and thinking skills. No mention was made of expectations regarding particular behavioral changes.

Effects of Program on Problem-Solving. The analyses of effects on thinking employed both analysis-of-variance and planned-comparison statistics. From these analyses it was possible to determine whether the training program was effective and whether the effectiveness was differential as a function of the behavior of the youngsters before training.

As a function of training, all three behavioral groups significantly enhanced their ability to conceptualize many alternative solutions to problems ($F = 106.90$, $p < 0.001$). This improvement was particularly marked among the two aberrant (impulsive and inhibited) groups of children ($F = 21.07$, $p < 0.001$). This improvement could not be ascribed to a mere increase in verbosity as a consequence of the program. An independent measure of superfluous or extraneous talk indicated that the program significantly decreased this kind of verbalization ($F = 21.86$, $p < 0.001$). This effect of decreasing extraneous talk was particularly striking among inhibited children because inhibited children who received no training actually increased in such talk during the control period. The training improved the quality of language and thought as well as the amount. This was further confirmed with an analysis of the program's effect on the ratio of relevant to total solutions each child thought of. Training significantly increased the proportion of relevant solutions given $(F = 9.98, \; p = 0.002)$, a measure that intrinsically controls for sheer amount of thought output. The training program thus not only increased the variety of alternative relevant solutions the child could imagine but also increased the degree to which his thinking was relevant to the problem faced.

Regarding quality of thought another measure was derived from the PIPS test: the force ratio, which is the ratio of solutions involving coercive, commanding, or hitting behavior to the total solutions offered. This was of interest because earlier studies suggested that although adjusted children think of forceful solutions as do maladjusted children, adjusted children can also think of other solutions and may give them higher priority. The data indicate that as a consequence of the program trained children significantly decreased in their force ratios whereas control children significantly increased during the same period $(F = 13.54, \; p < 0.001)$. Furthermore the decrease among trained children was most striking in the impulsive subgroup, children most likely to manifest such behavior. A further analysis was made of the order in which children thought of forceful and nonforceful solutions to problems. The order in which the child gave such solutions was taken to signify the priority given to them in thinking. Although 61 percent of trained children gave a forceful solution first before training, there was a significant decrease to 35 percent after training $(CR = 3.11, \; p < 0.01)$. Among control children 48 percent gave a forceful solution first at pretesting; significantly more (66 percent) control children gave a forceful solution first after the program had ended $(CR = 2.09, \; p < 0.05)$. These data suggest that the program may reverse a trend among inner-city preschoolers to think in terms of forceful solutions to typical interpersonal problems. This is of particular interest because the program does not teach the adult to reinforce or punish the children's ways of solving problems. In fact the program encourages children to think of all kinds of solutions to problems (for example, "Yes, that's one thing you might do. Now, can you think of another thing you might do?").

The findings regarding consequential and cause-and-effect thinking, although less extensive, essentially supplement and corroborate those regarding alternative thinking. The training program significantly enhanced the training group's ability to see different consequences to hypothetical acts ($F = 23.80$, $p < 0.001$). Although this effect occurred in all three groups it was particularly striking among children in the two aberrant-behavior groups ($F = 5.86$, $p = 0.02$). It was also possible to assess changes in the relevancy of consequences in a fashion similar to that described earlier with alternative thinking. Although they do not quite reach statistical significance ($p = 0.06$) the results suggest a definite trend for the training program to enhance the relevancy of conceptualized consequences as well as their sheer number. A separate measure of mere verbosity in response to the testing procedure indicates that these positive findings regarding consequential thinking cannot be ascribed simply to change in verbosity.

The training program also significantly enhanced the inclination of children to see causal connections in interpersonal events ($F = 6.70$, $p < 0.01$), particularly among children initially inhibited in behavioral adjustment. As with the other cognitive measures sheer amount of verbosity did not explain away the significance of the findings.

Thus data indicate that this training program has four major effects. First, it enhances alternative, consequential, and cause-and-effect thinking. Second, it decreases superfluous and irrelevant thinking. Third, it enhances problem-solving ability most among those who need it the most (those who are behaviorally aberrant). Fourth, it shifts the priority away from aggressive solutions and trains children to see nonforceful as well as forceful possibilities.

Effects of Training on Behavioral Adjustment. Because the purpose of this mental health program is to alter the behavioral adjustment of children through problem-solving skills, the major test of efficacy had to be whether or not behavioral adjustment changed in a positive direction.

Before the training period children were rated by their teachers on standard and reliable overt behavioral scales; these ratings served as a basis for classifying each child as impulsive, inhibited, or adjusted. The training and control groups were roughly equated in behavioral composition before the program. Before training, 36 percent of the trained group were classified as adjusted.

After training, there was a significant increase to 71 percent
(CR = 5.23, $p < 0.01$). Forty-seven percent of the untrained control children were judged adjusted before training and 54 percent
afterwards (no significant control group change). A detailed appreciation of the effect of the program on adjusted, impulsive, and
inhibited children considered separately is provided by Table 1.

Table 1 shows that of the ninety-one children rated as adjusted before training, forty-one were trained and fifty were not. Of
the forty-one trained children thirty-seven (90 percent) were again
rated as adjusted after training. Four (10 percent) of those forty-one
children rated as adjusted initially were rated as impulsive after
training and none as inhibited. Of the fifty adjusted children in the
control group forty-three (86 percent) remained adjusted.

The effect of the program can be seen in what happened to
children who started out impulsive and inhibited. Of the forty-four
who started out impulsive in the training group twenty-two (50 percent) were classified as behaviorally adjusted after the program. Of
the thirty-nine impulsive children in the control group only eight
(21 percent) were subsequently adjusted behaviorally ($\chi^2 =6.56$,
$p < 0.02$). Of the twenty-eight trained children who started out inhibited twenty-one (75 percent) ended up behaviorally adjusted.
This was true of only six (35 percent) of the seventeen children in
the control group ($\chi^2 = 5.39$, $p < 0.05$). The effects of the training
program were evident, whichever maladjusted group was considered.

Not only was the effect of training significant when trained
children were compared with control children but the McNemar
test for the significance of changes showed that the percentage of
trained children who moved from an aberrant to an adjusted category was significant for the training group considered alone. The
impact of the program could also be tested by examining how children moved between adjusted and maladjusted categories. Among
children exposed to training, only four of the forty-one (10 percent)
who began adjusted moved into an aberrant category; forty-three of
seventy-two (58 percent) moved from an aberrant into the adjusted
category ($\chi^2 = 30.72$, $p < 0.001$). Trained children as a group
tended to move from aberrant to adjusted. No such shift occurred
among control children ($\chi^2 = 1.72$, $p = NS$).

The effect of the training program on the behavioral adjust-

TABLE 1.

Effects of the Training Program on Different Kinds of Children

Post-Training Social-Adjustment	Pre-Training Social Adjustment					
	Adjusted (N = 91)		Impulsive (N = 83)		Inhibited (N = 45)	
	Training Group (N = 41)	Control Group (N = 50)	Training Group (N = 44)	Control Group (N = 39)	Training Group (N = 28)	Control Group (N = 17)
Adjusted	37 (90%)	43 (86%)	22 (50%)	8 (21%)	21 (75%)	6 (35%)
Impulsive[a]	4 (10%)	6 (12%)	22 (50%)	31 (79%)	2 (7%)	2 (12%)
Inhibited[a]	0 (0%)	1 (2%)	0 (0%)	0 (0%)	5 (18%)	9 (53%)
	$\chi^2 = 0.09$[b]		$\chi^2 = 6.56$[b]		$\chi^2 = 5.39$[b]	
	d.f. = 1		d.f. = 1		d.f. = 1	
	p = NS		$p < 0.02$		$p < 0.05$	

[a] These categories were combined in calculating χ^2.
[b] Yates' correction of continuity was applied to all chi squares.

ment of children is clear. The evidence suggests that youngsters who began the program adjusted remained so. Those who began the training program maladjusted tended to improve; this improvement was more striking among children who were initially inhibited.

As noted earlier four other behaviors had been shown to correlate with the problem-solving cognitive measures and were thus used to assess the effect of the training program.

The first of these behaviors was concern for others, defined as behaviors indicating concern for another child's feelings and willingness to help another child in distress. Analyses of variance indicated a significant triple interaction, suggesting that the training program significantly increased such behavior but not equally among all types of children. Separate analyses for each of the three groups of children indicated that such behaviors increased significantly only among children initially inhibited $(F = 6.53, p < 0.01)$. The training program increased the frequency with which initially inhibited children demonstrated empathic interest in their peers and willingness to reach out to them with help.

Because earlier data indicated sex differences in the relationship between problem-solving ability and being liked by peers, tests of the effect of the training program on such behavior were run on each sex separately. The second behavior, being liked by peers, was defined as being sought out by other children and the fact that others enjoy being with the child. No training effect emerged in the analyses of the boys' data. For girls, however, a significant positive training effect emerged $(F = 4.11, p = 0.04)$. A refined analysis indicated that this increase in being liked by peers was specific to girls who began as either impulsive $(F = 8.96, p = 0.004)$ or inhibited $(F = 8.83, p = 0.004)$. No change in being liked appeared in their respective control groups. Thus the training program was found to increase the likelihood with which girls would be sought out, especially those initially manifesting aberrant behavior. That no such finding emerged with boys is consistent with correlational data that indicated sex differences in the relation between problem-solving ability and being liked.

The third behavior, initiative, was simply rated on a scale of "shows initiative in what he does." Despite this general statement the findings on training effects were quite significant. Analyses of

variance indicated that training enhanced initiative among children
($F = 6.42$, $p < 0.01$) and that this positive effect occurred for all
three groups of children, especially the two aberrant groups.

The fourth behavior, autonomy, was defined as the child's
ability to complete activities by himself and overcome obstacles in
carrying out a task without apparent need for adult assistance. Data
indicated that training significantly increased autonomy ($F = 5.25$,
$p = 0.02$) and that the increase was evident among children initially
rated as adjusted, impulsive, and inhibited to the same extent.

The overt behavioral adjustment data thus indicated that
beyond enhancing the problem-solving skills of young children, the
twelve-week program also improved the overt behavioral adjustment
of the children involved. This improvement was most marked among
initially aberrant children most in need of such improvement but
was also manifest in children well within the normal range. Sixty
percent of the children who began the training program aberrant
were behaving normally after training. This was true of only 25
percent of the aberrant children who were not trained. Both the
impulsive and the inhibited groups of children were helped. Whenever differences in degree of help emerged, the data indicated that
symptom decrease was especially noticeable among inhibited children.

*Relation Between Problem-Solving and Behavioral Adjust-
ment.* Although the main purpose of the training program is to
improve the behavioral adjustment of children it has also furnished
evidence that behavioral change has occurred as a consequence of
cognitive change. The fact that overt behavioral change has been
demonstrated on three occasions as a consequence of the cognitive
training program is of course quite encouraging. It was even more
encouraging to discover in both preliminary studies that the degree
of overt behavioral change correlated significantly with the amount
of cognitive change produced by training.

For this reason the relation between the overt behavioral
change and the change in cognitive problem-solving ability with
training was examined once again in this comprehensive study. The
five inhibited children and twenty-two impulsive children who remained unchanged in their behavioral classification were combined
statistically into one group. Their cognitive change scores were compared with the combined change of the twenty-one initially inhibited

and twenty-two initially impulsive children whose behavior classification changed to adjusted. The prediction was that those forty-three children who shifted from aberrant to adjusted would show significantly greater enhancement in problem-solving ability than the twenty-seven who remained aberrant even though all showed some enhancement. It was also predicted that alternative thinking would relate most to behavioral change and least to cause-and-effect thinking because pretest correlations between these variables were of this order. It was also predicted that consequential thinking would relate to behavioral change, but weakly. This result was expected because the predictive power of consequential thinking to behavior had been shown to rest mainly on its distinguishing between impulsive and inhibited children. Because there were only five inhibited children who remained aberrant after training and these were combined for statistical purposes with those who remained impulsive, the specific relationship of consequential thinking to behavior change was being masked by the analyses.

As predicted, the strongest finding emerged in the test relating behavioral improvement to degree of enhanced alternative thinking. Trained children who began aberrant and ended up adjusted increased more in their PIPS scores than those who remained aberrant ($t = 6.78$, $p = 0.005$). Consequential thinking reached borderline significance ($t = 1.60$, $p = 0.06$; one-tailed test) whereas causal thinking failed to reach significance. The findings confirmed those of preliminary studies, indicating that altering those cognitive problem-solving skills most related to behavioral adjustment improves behavioral adjustment. The evidence supports the notion that the training program improves behavioral adjustment because it enhances problem-solving ability.

Follow-Up Study. The comprehensive study afforded the opportunity to follow up some trained and control children to examine the longevity of the program's positive effects. This is an important issue because other forms of early intervention in childhood have very temporary positive effects, a fact which requires that serious consideration be given to continued special programing.

The posttesting in the Get Set program took place in the spring of 1972. The behavioral adjustment of a sample of these children, some trained and some controls, was reevaluated soon after they entered kindergarten. Thus the spring, summer, and early fall of 1972 had elapsed between the end of the program and the follow-up evaluation. Also intervening during this period was a school strike in Philadelphia that interrupted the usual kindergarten period. The kindergarten teachers made overt-behavior ratings without knowing which children had had previous training. The ratings afforded data through which each child could again be classified as impulsive, inhibited, or adjusted, this time in the new kindergarten classroom.

Three analyses were made of the follow-up data, two of which allowed statistical tests of significance. The first did not allow the application of statistics because the samples chosen for comparison were highly selective. The idea was to compare trained and control children who started Get Set aberrant and became adjusted. Because only eight untrained children showed such improvement, no control group of sufficient size was available for statistical testing. It was still encouraging to note, however, that of the thirty-six trained follow-up children who had changed from aberrant to adjusted thirty were still classified as adjusted six months later.

Of the fifty-eight trained children who were classified as adjusted at the end of the training program (irrespective of their starting points), fifty (86 percent) were classified as adjusted six months later. This was true of only twenty-three of the thirty-five control children (66 percent) who were classified as adjusted at the end of the program (CR = 2.27, $p < 0.05$). These data indicated that program effects were maintained for at least a period of months without program reinforcement. Over the same period of months, the trained children as compared with controls also maintained their superior ability to conceptualize alternative solutions to problems and their consequences.

The third follow-up test came closest to an assessment of the program's primary preventive mental health impact. Examination of follow-up cases revealed twenty-seven trained and twenty-seven untrained children who had been classified as adjusted both at pre- and posttesting. The question was whether significantly more adjusted children who had undergone training would maintain their normalcy six months later than children who had not had the benefit of the program. Analysis indicated that twenty-five of the twenty-seven trained children (93 percent) remained adjusted six months later whereas only eighteen of the twenty-seven control children (67 percent) remained adjusted, a difference that is statiscally significant (CR = 2.37, $p < 0.05$).

The six-month follow-up results are encouraging. They indicate that obvious behavioral improvement as a consequence of training is not merely a temporary phenomenon. The alterations in thinking that occur with training become part of the child's repertoire for coping with his day-to-day problems. Furthermore, the data suggest that even the apparently adjusted child benefits from the program because the thinking processes he has already developed as an aid in coping are enhanced and reinforced by training, decreasing the chances that he will later become maladjusted. These results are particularly encouraging because follow-up data were obtained from new teachers who were naïve about the previous work with these children and in a kindergarten setting in many respects different from the Get Set child-care setting. Despite the changes in time period, raters, and setting, the positive effects of training persisted.

Summary of Findings

In considering the evaluative research data on program effectiveness one must keep in mind that the positive effects resulted from a specific course of training preschool children over a twelve-week period. It is reasonable to assume that had the program been an integral aspect of the Get Set program for a longer time, more children would have benefited and the benefits would have been even more obvious six months later because of the addition of more sophisticated games or prolonged use of the program style throughout the year. Only more research can reveal how intensive such training must be to produce a maximal positive effect over a given period of time. We do know that the program is feasible for child-care centers, is well received by teachers, and works. Current research is evaluating the effect of extending the program into kindergarten.

The research data also indicate that the program does something for children with behavioral problems, especially those who are inhibited. Practical questions are often asked by teachers and administrators about who needs the program and who does not. The answer is that as a secondary preventive program it works most efficiently for children who are inhibited, socially withdrawn, or afraid to express themselves. If only a handful of such children could be worked with, maximal gain would be noticeable. But the program also works for the impulsive and impatient child and apparently has a preventive effect on the behaviorally adjusted child.

The breadth of applicability is reinforced by other evidence. Analysis of training effects as a function of the IQ level of the child indicates that children of low average intelligence get as much out of the program as children who are bright. Although this is a cognitive training program its utility is not limited to a specific group on the basis of measured, impersonal cognitive ability. Those who are slow benefit, and those who are bright benefit. Furthermore no relationship was found between IQ change and change in problem-solving ability or change in behavioral adjustment as a function of training. The program enhances the quality of interpersonal problem-solving and behavioral adjustment independent of measured intelligence. As yet we do not know the level of intellectual ability below which the program is ineffective (mental subnormality)'.

The data also support the theory of why behavioral adjustment improves as a function of training. The evidence indicates that certain problem-solving abilities mediate behavioral adjustment and that enhancing these abilities enhances behavioral adjustment to the extent they are implicated. At this point the ability to concepualize relevant alternaive solutions to real-life problems bears the strongest relationship to adjustment; a secondary factor is consequential thinking. The place of social causal thinking in the scheme of things is less clear and requires further study.

The present evidence also suggests how relevant thinking guides and regulates behavioral adjustment. The program does not merely inhibit maladaptive behavior as might be suggested by the fact that a variety of impulsive and impatient behaviors diminish in frequency. Not only do impulsive children become less so but inhibited children become socially outgoing and exhibit adaptive and assertive behaviors. The evidence suggests also that the program enhances the modulating and regulating capacity of autonomous problem-solving. The flexible element in play here is clear: in some instances effective problem-solving suggests that one take action in an assertive way; in other instances it suggests that one avoid a certain action because of its consequences or because something better has come to mind. The effectiveness of such thinking, although it requires certain linguistic concepts and cognitive skills, does not appear to be predicated on learning specific solutions to specific problems. Instead its essence seems to be in assisting the child to think up his own options and their consequences. In this sense the child is taught how to think but not what to think.

This program has passed two stringent tests of efficacy. First it has not only shown it can improve the thinking skills of importance in adjustment but has gone one step further to show it can affect the ultimate criterion—overt behavioral adjustment. The few other studies in this field have demonstrated that it is possible to alter thought processes, but they have failed to demonstrate that such change has in any way altered actual behavioral adjustment outside the testing situation.

Second the program has been shown to alter actual behavioral adjustment beyond the physical and interpersonal setting of the training session. This generalization means that the positive program effects are not limited to a highly specialized, time-limited, training environment. What has been altered is not specific to one situation. It enhances adjustment throughout the school day, over time, and in the eyes of more than one adult. More information about the generalization of effects is presented in Chapter Eight.

8

Teacher and Parent Reports

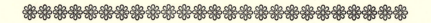

$\mathbb{S}$pontaneous reports from teachers about the children in the program have been consistent with the research findings indicating improvements in thinking and behavior. The responses of parents when interviewed informally have indicated that these changes were evident not only in the classroom but also in the home environment, having carried over into relations with family members.

Changes in Thinking

Teachers reported that many of the concepts taught formally were used by the children during the remainder of the school day. Typical was one child showing another child some pictures from a book and saying: "This bird is *different* from that one" or "This boy is *sad because* he's crying."

It was significant to note teacher comments regarding change in rate of verbal responsiveness during the formal training periods. Teacher reports were consistent both years the teachers ran the program. Children who generally did not speak much did not respond initially to the verbal portions of the formal training even though they may have responded to the physical portions of the program (such as tapping knees). After using the techniques described earlier to help the nonresponder they occasionally responded when only one or two words were necessary. At about the end of the fourth week most of these children began responding, in much the same way and at about the same point in the script each of the three years the program was conducted. During the problem-solving section of the program the extreme nonresponders began verbalizing by simply repeating what another child had just said. At first the teachers did not push for a different idea but praised the children for having said something. This imitation generally continued until about the sixth problem, when suddenly they would come up with a new idea of their own. In almost every case new ideas continued to flow once the children gave their own ideas. As one teacher said, "You can just tell by looking at him that he feels good about it."

By the end of the formal training period the children were not so quick to say, "I don't know." When asked a question both in and out of the formal training session the children seemed to think longer about the question before giving an answer or saying, "I don't know."

Changes in Overt Behavior

During development of the training program the teachers were not told that the ultimate goal of the program was to change overt behavior. Spontaneous reports of behavioral change thus impressed the investigators as further evidence of program effectiveness.

Much of the overt behavioral change reported by teachers and aides was congruent with changes in the thinking of the children as previously reported. Some teachers were particularly impressed that the children would tell them how they felt and why whereas previously they would whine or pout when frustrated. Such com-

munication is exemplified by Johnny, who asked for the play dough
at an inconvenient time. Instead of his typical whine, "but I want it
now," he said, "Now I'm sad." The teacher responded, "Can you
think of something *different* to do now that would make you feel
happy?" Johnny thought for a moment (a big step in itself for him)
and said, "I'll go paint." A child who had been hit would tell the
teacher about it and in some cases even say to the child who hit
him, "That makes me sad." The children were using tools to open
the way for communication with others and better resolution of their
problems.

One girl said to a classmate, "You're ugly, you got plaits."
Instead of reacting impulsively or showing emotional upset, she replied, "My hair is *different* from yours." Other teachers reported
similar reactions by children who were in some way belittled by
another child.

A boy who had bossed his way into getting what he wanted
was heard in a conversation with a girl in a wagon:

GIRL (*after the boy sat in the wagon*): Get out of here!
BOY: I want to sit here.
GIRL: I don't like you.
BOY: Why?
GIRL: You're too big.
BOY: If I pull you will you pull me?
GIRL: I can't pull you, you're too big.
BOY: If I pull you for a long time, will you let me sit in the wagon?
GIRL: OK.

The problem was solved by the boy completely on his own with no
direct teacher guidance.

Most of the children could not carry this type of problem-
solving to completion without some adult guidance. In fact even
with adult guidance similar to that described in Chapter Five the
impact of the program was not evidenced until the very end. Usually
it took time and patience on the part of the teacher before the children could use the concepts with spontaneity. These techniques do
not work overnight nor do they provide a quick and magic formula
for changing behavior. Given a modest amount of patience the
teacher (or other adult) can guide the child into using tools to do

his own thinking. At this point he is likely to use these tools to guide and control his behavior.

Comments of Teachers

During the training period teachers offered unsolicited comments about the program. The most consistent feeling was that the program had a definite goal which seemed realistic: that of teaching the child how to think. Some teachers appreciated the security of a well-planned curriculum and the explanations of how each lesson related to the preceding lesson. With regard to the informal dialogues used throughout the day the teachers found it difficult at first to guide a child to do his own thinking. As one teacher said, "I kept finding myself telling Steven not to grab toys, that he wouldn't like it if someone snatched his toys. If he persisted I would firmly say, 'Steven, grabbing is not allowed in this classroom'." After several conscious attempts the teacher commented that it soon became second nature to guide the children rather than tell them what to do and that she was impressed with how the children reacted.

A check was made to determine whether the teachers had become aware in using the script that a major goal of the program was to change overt behavior. Each teacher was asked to write a short paragraph at the end of the program telling what she thought the goals were. A typical response follows:

This training program I used most valuably to: First, describe the basic emotions; to verbalize them and to construct a superstructure by which the children could classify and then give content to their own feelings (to sort them out). The method of doing this was to teach connective words and to extend an environment of "permissiveness" for this verbalization and acting out of emotions.

Second, it was to bring out the differences of emotional reactions to given situations and in the process to awaken children to each others' feelings.

Third, to introduce the idea that any action that might be taken would have a consequence and that the child would bear a responsibility for his action.

Cognitive skills follow. As a child learns to accept and feel comfortable with emotionality, his mind is freed to become involved in real learning which is never "taught to him" but is discovered by spontaneous interest on his part from (emotions→ external world) inside and out.

Goals of the program may have been to increase intellectual skills by making the children more verbal (as is often found in white middle-class children). However, without first allowing understanding of one's feelings this cannot be accomplished.

Most teachers wrote similar notes; some simply described the cognitive lessons of the program. No teacher mentioned behavioral change as a program goal. Although the teacher quoted above felt that emotions must be freed she was clearly unaware of the specific research hypothesis concerning specific behaviors that would improve as a function of increasing cognitive problem-solving skills.

Comments of Parents

Although parents were informed at the beginning of the year that their children would be in an experimental training program they were only aware that the program involved an experiment to teach thinking skills. To ensure that there would not be differential reinforcement or lack of it at home, they were not told about details of the training during the research period. At the end of the training twenty mothers were asked specific questions about their child's behavior at home. These questions were not meant to supply research data but merely to explore the possibility that effects of training carried over into the home. Some typical comments from the mothers in response to particular questions follow.

Compared to a few months ago, say about November, does your child use the words same *or* different *at home more, less, or about the same? If more, can you give an example?*

One mother replied that one night at the dinner table her child picked up a cup and said, "A cup is *different* from a saucer. A spoon is *different* from a knife." Another mother offered that her son said, "Meat is *different* from potatoes." A third child said, "We are all eating the *same* thing." In each instance the words *same* and *different* were used with emphasized voice inflections. During the day the teachers often engaged in similar conversations at juice and lunch time, and some children spontaneously initiated this kind of discussion at home. A child would be heard saying to her friend, "Your toy is *different* from mine."

When asked if they were surprised to hear the changes in their child's talk parents consistently reported that they were. Though unaware that games using these words were part of the training program the mothers did assume, however, that their children learned the words *same* and *different* at school.

Does your child tell you how he feels? That is, does he use the words happy, sad, *or* mad *more, less, or about the same? If more, can you give an example?*

One mother replied that her son had recently started to tell her how he felt. If he was given something he wanted he would say "That makes me happy," and if he could not have what he wanted he would say "I'm sad." When asked if the latter made her give in the mother said: "Not usually, but one time he wanted me to buy him a candy bar and he used to whine and be a terrible pest when I said no. The other day he just said 'I'm sad' and gave me those big eyes and I just couldn't say no. So I got it for him and he said, 'Now I'm happy.' I couldn't believe it. He seemed so calm." The mother was then asked how that made her feel and she replied, with a big smile, "Real good."

Does your child use such words as happy, sad, *or* mad *in reference to your feelings more, less, or about the same? If more, can you give an example?*

Nearly all the mothers interviewed responded enthusiastically to this question. One boy was reported as running down the stairs, hugging his mother, and saying, "I just want to make you happy, Mommy." One mother reported that her child never picked up her toys but one day picked up all her toys and said, "Are you happy, Mommy? I picked up all my toys." Another child said to his mother, who had a headache, "Are you sad, Mommy? I'll make you feel better," and kissed her. Still another looked at his mother and asked, "Mama, why are you mad?" The mother said, "I'm not mad," and the boy responded, "You look mad."

*Does your child behave or talk differently to his brothers
and sisters or neighborhood children? For example, if someone has
something that he wants or in how much he fights?*

The question was answered with enthusiasm. One mother
reported that her son had become much more sensitive to the
feelings of his little brother Anton, aged two and one-half. "When
Anton is crying Johnny often says, 'why are you so sad?' and asks
him to play with him. One day he was heard saying, 'Anton, I
want to make you happy,' and another time he was very upset
because I kissed him and I didn't kiss Anton too."

Several mothers indicated that when their child's younger
brothers or sisters cry they might try to make them laugh by saying,
"Do you want to play with this toy?", or pat them on the head, or
say, "Why are you crying? Why are you so sad?"

Besides sensitivity about feelings one mother reported:
"James has really grown up when it comes to Jennifer (his two-
year-old sister). If she had something he wanted he'd just snatch
it right out of her hands. Now he asks her for it." The mother was
then asked what happened if Jennifer would not let James have it.
"Then he comes and tells me. The other day he said, 'Jennifer
had it for a long time and now it's my turn.' " The mother said
she had never heard him say anything like that before. She added
that at times he still snatched things from her if he wanted them
badly enough but now he usually asked for things. One mother
mentioned that her child still grabs things from his younger brother,
but if he cries he now says, "OK, you can keep it." Previously he
did not seem concerned whether his younger brother cried or not.
Another mother said that when her son wants something from his
younger brother he will first ask, but if his brother says no he
will grab it. If his brother cries he says he doesn't care because he
asked him first. All these behaviors revealed, in the mother's eyes,
some change from previous behavior.

One mother related a dialogue between herself and her child
describing how he handled a situation in which Wayne, a neighborhood boy, hit him. She noted that Steven had always been afraid
of Wayne, who is two years older and considerably bigger than
Steven.

STEVEN: Mama, Wayne hit me!

MOTHER: Go and tell his mother.

STEVEN: I did. She didn't give him no whoopin'.

MOTHER: Then go hit him back.

STEVEN: I can't, he's too big. (*Steven then went out, was gone a long time, and returned.*)

MOTHER: Where did you go so long?

STEVEN: I was out playin' with Wayne.

MOTHER: Was he fighting?

STEVEN: No, I told him if he don't hit me no more, he could have some candy.

MOTHER: Did you give him candy?

STEVEN: Yep, and he don't hit me no more.

The mother reported that Steven and Wayne played and were friends for two days. The mother did not guide the child in the style of the training program; she suggested what her son might do: go tell his mother, go hit him back, and so forth. Although Steven was still afraid to hit Wayne back he was able to solve the problem on his own in a different way by thinking of an effective way to persuade Wayne to stop hitting him. The mother was pleased to see that Steven was now able to play with Wayne even though she was not aware that he was reacting to a training program in problem-solving skills at school.

Another mother noticed that her child had recently begun telling his older brother (aged six): "If you be good, Mommy might take us to the movies," and "If you climb on those steps like that, you might fall and then you be sad." This advice shows use of the consequential thinking skills the children learned as part of the training program. Another mother noticed her child telling her little sister, "If you are *not* good, Mommy might spank you," and "Mommy does *not* like that." The word *not* was stressed throughout training as a prerequisite tool in problem-solving skills. The mother offered the quotes, however, without being asked directly about the child's use of the word *not*.

Mothers also noticed that when they bought their children little things at a drugstore or grocery store they would ask if they could get some for their sister or brother or friends. Most mothers replied that they did not pay attention to the requests at the time.

One mother did ask why her child wanted some gum for his friend and got the reply: "Because it will make him happy." The mother added that when her child said that, she was so surprised she could not say no.

When your child cannot have something that he wants or when you are angry or displeased with him, does he react any differently than he did a few months ago? If yes, can you give an example?

One mother said that her son used to throw a temper tantrum and go into his room if he could not have something he wanted. He did not do this anymore. Another said that if her child could not have something he wanted he would simply say OK. Now he says things like: "I guess I just can't have that balloon" and keeps looking at it. Then he adds, "That balloon is so pretty." And then, "It would make me so happy if I could have that balloon. I could put it right in my room." The mother laughed when reporting this, adding: "How could I say no to that? He really maneuvered me." When asked how she felt about it her reply was, "It's OK, but I don't always give in. Sometimes I just have to put my foot down, but he takes it OK."

Most mothers felt that their children now attempt to explain when they make their mother angry. One child was reported to have said, "Let me tell you why I hit Jimmy." The child's mother said she finds herself listening more to her child because "he talks to me more now." Another child broke a vase and the mother thought he did it on purpose. Her child explained that his little brother pushed him and that he would glue it together. The mother knew he would not really be able to glue it but was so touched that she found herself unable to get angry.

Some mothers reported that when their children do something they know they will be punished for, they now tell their mothers about it first. Most typical are confessions or such statements as "I did it." One mother was quite surprised when her son came to her one day and said, "I spilled the sugar on the floor and I cleaned it all up." She said that in the past he would have just left it there and denied having done it.

One mother said, "Now if I get angry at Deborah she gets all lovey-dovey and kisses me." When asked how she felt about that her answer was: "Sometimes I like it but sometimes I get madder because I really want to punish her." When asked how Deborah acts at those times the mother said, "One time I wouldn't let her kiss me because I was really mad. But Deborah said, 'Would a big hug make you happy?' " The mother continued, "I was still angry, but what could I do when she said that?" In the same vein another mother said that when a kiss did not work her child would now say: "Do you like hugs?"

Are there any other interesting changes about your child's behavior or thinking as you see them at home that you would like to tell us about?

Some mothers responded that their children seem much happier and do not pout and whine so much. As one mother put it: "He's not such a pest anymore." The children were reported to be more concerned about other people's feelings; this change was most apparent among those who had younger brothers and sisters.

The reports of mothers by no means constitute proof that what was learned in the training program carried over into the home. We were quite impressed, however, with the likelihood that such generalization did in fact take place. Mothers reported changes in behavior and use of language remarkably similar to changes noted in the classroom. Reported changes in ability to tolerate frustration and control emotions closely match the changes in behavior measured in the research evaluation of the program.

The reports of teachers and mothers constitute interesting information in other respects. The changes in thinking and subsequent overt behavior made the children more likeable and better able to satisfy their wishes than before. And as better problem-solvers they elicited more positive feelings from adults and seemed better able to make and maintain good peer relations. Perhaps adults especially value verbalization in a child because it makes the child's behavior understandable and appear more reasonable. In any case the children in the training program improved in their ability to explain themselves to adults, both by making their own needs known and in expressing awareness of the relationship between themselves and others.

Perhaps of greatest potential significance is the suggestion in these informal reports, supporting the research evidence, that training of certain intermediary thought processes enhances the capacity to solve problems in general. Certainly the goal of any treatment or intervention program is to affect behavior across a range of situations, not merely within the treatment or intervention situation.

The reports of teachers and parents, as well as the measured changes in behavior reported earlier, suggest that by learning how to think when confronted with interpersonal problems the growing child acquires skills applicable in a broad range of situations that enhance the likelihood of subsequent social success and good feeling.

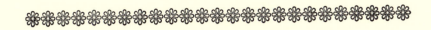

9

Putting the
Program into Effect

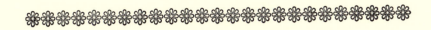

Although the program script is designed to be a self-contained package for anyone who wishes to use it and the dialogues in Chapters Five and Six are a guide for application throughout the day, the participating research teachers received a careful introduction to the program and regular supervision while learning to work with it. Because the techniques for training teachers would also be suitable for training mental health workers, residential treatment staff, and others involved with the education and guidance of groups of young children, a brief description of what took place in the training meetings with teachers should be useful. In any new program some training and ongoing initial consultation is always useful. Although all elements provided teachers during the research phase may not be necessary, attempts to institute this program in a new setting should provide as much training and support as possible.

Putting the training program into effect may also involve employing the evaluative measures and interacting with administrative personnel of the school or treating system. Our experience is offered for guidance.

Training and Consultation with Teachers

The first meeting with teachers was a brief orientation session lasting approximately an hour. Its purpose was to enlist interest and positive motivation and to explain the basic content and problem-solving goals of the program. The program was presented as a cognitive training curriculum; no mention was made of an intent to affect behavioral adjustment. Now that the program has been well researched it is perfectly feasible to say that the primary goal is to improve the behavioral adjustment of youngsters and to prevent behavioral difficulties in well-adjusted children through the training of real-life interpersonal problem-solving skills. During this meeting the teachers were introduced to the idea of a script, the basic word-concepts, and how the script is sequenced. They were told how each lesson leads to the next until the final problem-solving lessons are completed.

After this initial orientation the teachers met with the research staff for ten meetings, each lasting approximately three hours. The first meeting took place the week before the program began and was devoted to demonstrating the initial lessons. Each teacher acted the lessons out to ensure familarity with the games and dialogues before conducting them with the children. In addition each teacher was given a tape recorder so that sessions with the children could be heard and discussed in subsequent meetings if needed.

Beginning with the second meeting, any problems a teacher had had with a previous lesson were discussed, and any suggestions for change in content or method of presentation, if agreed upon, were implemented. Thus script refinement was a continuing process. Lessons for the following week were again demonstrated and acted out, and excerpts of tapes from the previous week were heard. After a few weeks not every teacher needed to act out every lesson, especially lessons that were similar to previous ones, but every lesson was demonstrated. Because of the time needed for discussions, role-playing, and listening to the tapes the teachers met in small groups of six or less.

Dialogues the teachers could apply informally throughout the day were also described during these meetings. These dialogues, similar to those presented in Chapter Six, were presented each week consistent with the concepts covered in the formal training lessons at hand.

Besides these weekly meetings with the teachers, three meetings were held with the teachers' aides. The aides did not conduct the formal training but were informed of the ostensible goals of the program and were given the dialogues to be used informally throughout the day. The aides were informed of the necessity of using these dialogues for consistency in the classroom and added exposure for the children. Aides were also told how they could help in the formal training, especially with respect to the disruptive and withdrawn children (see Chapter Three).

Finally the research staff made periodic visits to each classroom and observed training sessions. The teachers appreciated these visits because they provided an extra sense of security and the opportunity for helpful suggestions.

We suggest that inservice personnel or supervisors who train teachers or mental health staff in the use of the program hold weekly meetings. Ongoing support and supervision is probably more efficient than a thorough review of the script before working with the children for at least two reasons. First, unforeseen problems may arise that can best be dealt with when supervisors maintain continuous contact on a weekly basis. Second, each lesson is fresh in the trainer's mind when she conducts it just before applying it for the first time with the children. The weekly meetings also allow those being trained to express both the frustrations and the satisfactions they experienced during the previous week. If such meetings are not possible there is no reason to doubt that workshops held before the school year would work. Experience with shorter weekly sessions, however, has proved quite successful.

Evaluating the Program

Teachers who conduct the program receive daily feedback as they see how their children are progressing. However, school psychologists, program administrators, and mental health program directors in other settings may wish to evaluate the program systematically. The tests and measurements used in the research design are described in Chapter Twelve, and the tests and behavioral ratings may be obtained by writing to the authors.

The first test, the PIPS test, can be administered in twenty to thirty minutes depending on the child. The second test, the What Happens Next? game, measures consequential thinking and takes approximately the same length of time. For children who are in school or other programs all day, it is best to test in the morning when the children are most alert. We have found that if it is possible to test from 9 A.M. to noon a group of fifteen children can be tested on both tests in six days without interfering with the ongoing program.

The rating scales are designed for the teacher to complete after she has had at least one month to learn the behavior of the children. Each child should be rated quickly, the ratings taking no more than five minutes per child. For program evaluation the tests and behavioral ratings should be completed before and after training so that comparisons can be made. The teacher or administrator must determine how much, if any, formal evaluation to conduct, depending on the needs of her situation.

Neither the tests nor rating scales should be administered without examining them carefully and using them with a few children who will not be involved in the training program. Both the tests and the scales are straightforward measuring devices, but familiarity with them beforehand enhances the reliability and validity of the results.

Working with Administrators

Because it is often middle-level staff who institute new programs in schools or mental health settings, our experience in working with top-level administrators, school principals, and program supervisors may be of practical help to those who wish to make our approach part of their overall program. The need to provide training and orientation for those who use the program with children has been stressed. For the program to succeed, however, care must also be taken in working with those who bear ultimate responsibility for educational and mental health programing.

It is first important to obtain clearance and support for the program from top administrators. We obtained clearance from the director of research and the director of early childhood education in the school district of Philadelphia to approach the director of research of the Get Set day-care program of Philadelphia, through whom in turn the support of the director of the entire program was obtained. To achieve this it was necessary to prepare a clear statement of what the program would achieve for them, what the expense would be to them in effort and money, and how it would fit into their overall educational goals. Then the supervisors of each day-care center were approached with the knowledge that the program had the clearance and support of top-level administrators. It was important to explain to the supervisors what the program consists of, that it would in no way conflict with the ongoing goals of the existing program, and that the content would be congenial to the experience and needs of the teachers. It was crucial to provide the supervisors with details about the sequenced script to communicate how it is different in its totality from any of its elements that may already be taught. It was not unusual to get a quick reaction of "Oh, we do that already!" Those immediately responsible for programs hesitate to make changes unless convinced that the change has merit and will not cause a disturbance among staff. Only after this sequence of clearances and explanations was an approach to teachers made. Such care in touching every administrative base is well worth the effort. It shows respect for the authority and responsibility of these administrators and ensures their assistance if things go wrong.

Another important element is that of providing feedback to administrators and supervisors regarding the progress being made during the program, as well as final results. Administrators frequently complain that once they give clearance for a new program, they never hear about the program again until something goes wrong.

IO

Implications for
Future Research
and Practice

The research and resulting program derived from a conception of healthy human functioning that emphasizes the ability of an individual to solve everyday, interpersonal problems.

Our background research indicates that with young children a significant element in problem-solving is the ability to imagine alternative solutions. Another significant element is the ability to imagine alternative consequences to a social act. There is also evidence that the ability of nine- to twelve-year-old children to articulate the means in reaching a stated goal contributes to behavioral adjustment.

In some studies measures of these abilities relate modestly to measured IQ, but this relationship does not explain the significance of these problem-solving abilities for behavioral adjustment. In fact it has been shown that the more adjustment measures touch on social interaction in the classroom, the less IQ comes into play in any way. Furthermore these cognitive abilities do not merely reflect verbosity or willingness to talk during testing or the informal daily interchanges between adult and child. This problem-solving *style* of thought has significance for behavioral adjustment in young children irrespective of sex or socioeconomic level even though social class experiences may affect the development of problem-solving skills.

With the theory that cognitive interpersonal problem-solving skills mediate behavioral adjustment, a program was developed to train young children in order to enhance these skills. Repeatedly the evidence has supported what earlier was only a theory derived from the correlation between such thinking skills and behavioral adjustment. Controlled change in these thinking processes as a function of training has led to enhanced social adjustment, and it is now clear that it was the change in ability to solve problems that enhanced adjustment and not an extraneous set of factors implicit in the program. A direct link was suggested in the fact that the degree of behavioral change correlates with the degree of cognitive change. That is, trained youngsters who improved most in the trained cognitive skills also improved most in their overt behavioral adjustment. These changes in thinking and behavior persist over a period of months without exposure to a subsequent special training program of any sort. Also, children judged to be well adjusted before the program were found many months after the program to have maintained their adjustment with significantly greater likelihood than well-adjusted children who were not exposed to the program. The training thus constitutes a program of primary prevention in mental health. The power of the cognitive processes to mediate adjustment is further supported by the evidence that enhanced adjustment generalizes to situations outside the specific training program.

Both the current line of research and its potential for practical application justify continued effort. There are wide gaps in our current knowledge about problem-solving skills relevant to social adjustment, and only a beginning has been made in the numerous possibilities open for application. Background research suggests that the importance of this approach is not limited to the early years but in fact bridges a wide age range.

Implications for Young Children

Two elements comprising interpersonal problem-solving ability among young children are at this point well established: alternative and consequential thinking.

Alternative thinking has repeatedly emerged as a key ability and warrants careful study in its own right. One avenue of research might be to explore the linguistic prerequisites of alternative thinking. The training program teaches the word-concepts *and* and *not* on the basis that they are crucial to the development of alternative problem-solving ability. If the child creates alternatives in his mind, presumably it is on the basis of his being able to think: "I can do ——— *and* ———" or "I will do ——— but *not* ———." A measure of mastery of these concepts has in fact been shown to correlate with alternative (PIPS) thinking scores, and a discriminant analysis suggests that the relationship between mastery of the word-concepts *and* and *not* and behavioral adjustment is mediated by alternative thinking (Shure, Newman, and Silver, 1973). This finding supports the contention that mastery of these word-concepts is a prerequisite element in developing alternative problem-solving ability. Other direct links between alternative thinking and the word-concepts *or* and *same-different* have not been experimentally established as yet.

We know that alternative thinking influences social adjustment independently of measured intelligence. In fact there is evidence that among young children the capacity of IQ to predict adjustment versus maladjustment is totally subsumed by the predictive power of knowing the child's alternative thinking ability. We do not know whether alternative thinking reflects a broad, underlying ability among young children. It may be more than coincidental that the measures of alternative and consequential thinking which relate to social adjustment among young children require the child to articulate possibilities and that the training program places great emphasis on the child's providing his own questions and answers. The suggestion is that future research should examine the dimensions of thought underlying the problem-solving skills studied to date. Such a study has been done with adults and is discussed below; the adult data suggest just such a tendency to articulate problem-solving thoughts. Factor-analytic methodology might be one method of exploring dimensions that may underlie a number of measured problem-solving skills.

As suggested, consequential thinking relates to social adjustment in young children only when the situation focuses attention on alternative consequences. Having to produce alternative consequences, however, adds something to what is known about a child beyond his ability to produce alternative solutions to problems. For instance, this ability to imagine consequences is particularly deficient in inhibited children compared with both well-adjusted and impulsive children. Is it possible that the nonresponding which characterizes inhibited young children has limited their experience and therefore appreciation of the consequences that follow responding? In training impulsive youngsters we noted that such youngsters might grab or not wait their turn, causing a problem with their peers. However, they often indicated that they knew what might happen next (the consequences) but that this did not stop them. They acted aware of and in spite of the consequences. The evidence suggests that children with different behavioral patterns may be characterized by different patterns of interpersonal cognitive ability. With further articulation of the elements that constitute the problem-solving ability of children, one may be able to profile a child's problem-solving skills and apply remedial-educational methods suited to the pattern of cognitive deficit.

This possibility leads to the need to explore other problem-solving abilities in young children. The significance of causal thinking in social adjustment is less clear than alternative or consequential thinking. Young maladjusted children exhibit less tendency to think in terms of social causes than their adjusted peers (Shure, Newman, and Silver, 1973), but measures of causal thinking ability do not contribute more to prediction of adjustment beyond what alternative and consequential thinking already tell us. All studies to date have used a procedure that leads the person to think in terms of what might have caused a particular event but does not demand that he think of a cause. Again it may be necessary to devise a method of measuring the ability to think in terms of social cause and effect that will assess whether the child can adequately conceptualize in this fashion if he has to. A person may be able to think in a certain way, but may not unless he has to. A study with kindergarten children specifically draws the child's attention to the issue of why a hypothetical child acted as he did. With this procedure we will be able to assess each child's ability to see different categories when specifically asked for causes ("Why did Johnny hit George?"). The same study is exploring a measure of sensitivity of young children to the existence of a problem and the relationship of this sensitivity to behavioral adjustment. The children are shown pictures of people in problem situations and asked: "Oh-oh! Something is wrong . . . something happened . . . what's the matter?"

Although the ability to spell out the step-by-step means to achieve a personal goal relates to behavioral adjustment among older children and adults, the means-end testing procedure is beyond the ability of young children to handle. Their inability to tell the kind of story demanded by the task probably reflects their inability to think in such a sequenced and temporally organized fashion. Little is known, then, about the early emergence of this means-end ability except that it develops sometime between ages five and ten.

An unexpected finding is that the content of solutions thought of by young children differs as a function of overall problem-solving ability. It was no surprise to discover that children from different socioeconomic and cultural environments think differently about the use of force. It was a surprise to find that within such environments the less skillful problem-solvers more often think of force first than their better problem-solving peers. The relationship between style (number of solutions) and content (what solutions) remains to be explored. More is said about this issue in the next section, where we discuss findings from studies of adults.

At this point no data are available on the child-rearing experiences that may distinguish good and poor interpersonal problem-solvers. The fact that young children from different socioeconomic groups differ in problem-solving effectiveness may provide a lead, especially considering the fact that families from different socio-economic levels differ in how they handle problems as a family. Straus (1968) has described a unique study. Working-class families in Bombay, San Juan (Puerto Rico), and Minneapolis, were compared with middle-class families in the same culture on how they handled a problem presented to them as a family group. Straus discovered that the lower-class family's members worked in a more isolated fashion in their attempts to handle the situation. Family members were less prone to discuss the problem together, less often shared information about possible solutions to the problem, less often attempted to show one another what to do, and ended up with a narrower range of solutions.

Findings regarding the linguistic deficiences of many poor children may also be relevant insofar as they implicate the mother-child relationship. Hess and Shipman (1966) have been quite specific about the characteristics of mother-child interactions that lead the child to frustration and failure to develop linguistic skills. Some of these characteristics are the mother's inability to define a goal for or with the child, not giving specific directions to the child to help him with a problem, not guiding the child to a solution, and general inability to convey intent to the child in words. In reviewing the relation of early development to cognitive growth, Gray and Miller (1967, p. 483) note:

> *Hess and Shipman argued that the growth of cognitive processes is dependent on the cognitive meaning in the mother-child communication system. Impoverishment of meaning in the family communication and control system means* fewer available alternatives for considerations and choice. [*Emphasis added.*] *Unavailability of behavioral alternatives and restricting parent-child relationship militate against adequate cognitive growth. Interaction patterns which rely on status rules rather than attention to the characteristics of the specific situation, and where behavior fails to be mediated by verbal cues, tend to produce a child who relates to authority rather than rationale. A strong case for the pivotal point a mother plays in early cognitive development as an instrumental source of stimulation is made by such studies.*

We must emphasize that these studies have not dealt with

social problem-solving and repeat that the interpersonal problem-solving skills under consideration in this book have been shown to relate to social adjustment irrespective of socioeconomic level. Furthermore interpersonal problem-solving skills do not merely reflect verbosity, sheer quantity of thinking in general, or mental power insofar as measured intelligence is concerned. Nevertheless, if relative strangers can through training affect the interpersonal problem-solving of a child in less than three months, communication between parents and child must have a significant impact.

In looking for the child-rearing origins of effective problem-solving, it may also be fruitful to explore family attitudes regarding problems and how problems that arise are approached in the family. Are parents who feel powerless and afraid unable to teach children how to deal with problems because they themselves must avoid dealing with them? Are there benign differences between families that have implications for differences in offspring? Hertzig and others (1968) have shown how three-year-old children from culturally divergent families tackle problems quite differently. Some talk, others gesture; some are task-oriented, others are socially oriented; some talk irrelevantly when they fail, others do not. Minuchin, Chamberlain, and Granbard (1967) have shown that poor and disorganized families rarely communicate about problems in words and that the child learns it is the force and loudness of an argument which establishes validity and not its logic. There is little evidence at this moment, but it seems reasonable to assume that we learn styles of interpersonal problem-solving as these emerge in our commerce with people and that parents and other significant adults are teachers and models of these styles while interacting with children in the home, at the dinner table, in dealing with sibling rivalries, in settling marital disagreements, and whenever family members interact and discuss what is wrong and what ought to be done about it.

Having developed and validated a program for young children that enhances interpersonal problem-solving skills and subsequent behavioral adjustment, it is reasonable to examine both the program and its philosophy in more detail. The program has been conceived as educational in nature. A sequenced set of lessons is presented as a curriculum by teachers on the assumption that if children learn to think a certain way they will be able to cope with their social environment better than before. As such, elements of the program can be studied, some added or subtracted, and the effects measured. What the teacher (therapist?) does and says can be specified and taught.

The philosophy implicit in the program is that if one wishes to affect the behavior of people one must affect the specific (cognitive) abilities that mediate the behavior in question. The search has been and still is to discover the mediating cognitions intimately affecting social adjustment. No assumption has been made that there is a single problem-solving capacity or process. In a similar fashion McClelland (1973) argues against the usefulness of IQ or other general ability measures in predicting success in life outcomes. He also emphasizes (1973, p. 12) the need to focus on "operant thought patterns to get maximum generalizability to various action outcomes." Our program suggests that interpersonal problem-solving constitutes just such "operant thought patterns" when social adjustment is of concern.

In emphasizing the educative (cognitive) aspects of intervention, our approach suggests a broad potential for application. The script may be used as a core curriculum in nursery schools and child-care centers, and the approach is applicable system-wide if school administrators wish it. For instance one or two teachers or supervisors who become familiar with the program could train and supervise other teachers in the use of the program. Teachers who have used the script and general approach to children report that it has slowly but significantly changed their entire approach to handling their classes. The potential in the program for work with parents remains totally unexplored. Adaptation for use in the home seems well worth the effort considering the need for primary preventive approaches that have some proven efficacy.

Application of the program script with severely disturbed young children has not been attempted to date although there is nothing in the program to militate against such an effort. Certainly there is no reason why the dialogues and games described in Chapter Six could not be applied in therapeutic and educational interactions with children. In essence they define a way of relating to children, talking to them, and encouraging them to think about what they are doing, why, and its effects on others and themselves.

Implications for Older Children, Adolescents, and Adults

Alternative thinking is not only a significant skill in young children but has also been shown to differentiate groups of ten-year olds differing in adjustment level (Shure and Spivack, 1970a) and to differentiate hospitalized emotionally disturbed adolescents and adults from their normal peers (Platt, Altman, and Altman, 1973; Platt and Spivack, 1973b). Thus the capacity to think in terms of solutions to interpersonal problems is significant for adjustive capacity across a broad age range. A clue to what might underlie this ability, at least among adults, comes from a factor analysis of a number of problem-solving measures (Platt and Spivack, 1973b). The ability to provide alternative solutions and the ability to state a variety of problems defined one factor, which suggests the existence of a common element. Examining the two measures and contrasting them with others used but not included in this factor suggested that the common element might be the capacity to articulate possibilities when confronted with interpersonal problems. This finding suggests the possibility of a superordinate cognitive ability, such as open-mindedness or willingness (or ability) to explore without needing to find a quick answer in human affairs. Is this the converse of dogmatism?

The ability of older children and adults to conceptualize the consequences of social behavior has not been explored with a procedure that demands consequential thought. With procedures that present social situations, ask the person to tell about them, and then measure whether or not consequences are mentioned, scores have not discriminated ten-year olds differing in adjustment level (Larcen, Spivack, and Shure, 1972) nor psychiatrically hospitalized adolescents from a normal control group (Platt, Altman, and Altman, 1973). But scores with such a procedure have differentiated impulsive adolescents from normals (Spivack and Levine, 1963) and psychiatrically hospitalized adults from normal controls (Platt and Spivack, 1973b). These data suggest a developmental increase in the significance of the spontaneous tendency to think consequentially when one considers social adjustment. Young children and pre-teen-agers may not spontaneously think of consequences to the point where a differential level has any significance for adjustment. The significance of spontaneously thinking of consequences may emerge only during the adolescent years and find its importance in adulthood. Only thorough developmental studies can settle this issue.

The ability to articulate a set of steps that may solve a stated human problem (means-ends thinking) has been shown to relate to adjustment on numerous occasions and in widely disparate groups. Deficient performance on the means-ends cognitive task has identified less-adjusted ten-year olds (Larcen, Spivack, and Shure, 1972; Shure and Spivack, 1972b), adolescents and young adults (Spivack and Levine, 1963; Platt, Altman, and Altman, 1973; Platt, Scura, and Hannon, 1973), and adults (Platt and Spivack, 1972a, 1972b, 1973b). As already noted preschool children have not been able to respond to the procedure, which requires a story-telling ability beyond their capacity. Little is known, then, about the early emergence of this means-ends ability although it obviously requires the capacity to connect a sequence of events that will move one from a problem to its solution. Implied in this is the ability to see the complex relationships between events and people as one devises a plan of action. In the factor analysis of adult problem-solving referred to earlier, means-ends thinking and a measure of role-taking loaded on the same factor. The latter is said to measure the ability to see a social situation from more than one perspective, especially to appreciate another person's point of view (Feffer, 1970). The fact that this measure and means-ends thinking loaded on the same factor supports the notion that means-ends thinking demands more than most preschool children are capable of. Its presence and significance at age ten, however, indicate that it emerges sometime between the ages of nine and twelve and marks an important developmental step as far as adjustive capacity is concerned.

The spontaneous tendency to think of causes of interpersonal events has been shown to differentiate normal adults from psychiatrically hospitalized adults (Platt and Spivack, 1973b) but not normal adolescents from psychiatrically hospitalized adolescents (Platt, Altman, and Altman, 1973). As with the spontaneous consideration of consequences, spontaneous sensitivity to causes may only have significance for adjustment in the mature years. The significance for adjustment of the capacity to articulate causes when the situation demands it remains to be demonstrated. Similarly there remains the task of assessing whether sensitivity to the presence of interpersonal problems differentiates people who differ in social adjustment. In the studies of Platt, Altman, and Altman with adolescents and Platt and Spivack with adults, a measure attempting to get at this issue failed to differentiate hospitalized from normal groups. The task required the individual to tell, under a standard probing procedure, all the kinds of problems people typically have in life. Subjects classified as sensitive were those able to provide the most varied assortment of problems. It may very well be that an ingenious and subtle measure is needed to get at this ability or sensitivity if in fact there is such a skill that may be said to typify a person. Perhaps this area is refractory to straightforward exploration because psychological defense mechanisms protect the person from awareness of his problems. This fact would make sensitivity to (awareness of) a problem specific to the problem being focused on and its potential for arousing anxiety or discomfort. This possibility raises in turn the fact that we currently know nothing about the specific forces that influence the effectiveness with which a child or adult manifests his interpersonal problem-solving skills. Do anxiety or emotions hamper the operation of these skills, and if so in what ways and under what circumstances? Does one's level of personal involvement or motivation influence his problem-solving efficiency? Do certain social settings or types of interpersonal relationship enhance effective thinking?

As noted with young children the content of problem-solving thought is related to social adjustment among adults. Platt and Spivack (1973a) compared the means of psychiatric patients and normal adults to solve problems. When confronted with a problem the normals were significantly more likely than the patients in their stories to have their protagonist speak of a "plan," of "trying to figure out the problem," or of "learning what went wrong." The normal group's references to thinking about and through a problem were in contrast to those of the patients, whose protagonist was usually described as doing something concrete in the situation.

This tendency among the well adjusted to state explicitly the need to plan or think through what could be done was true of normals differing widely in cultural background. It has also been demonstrated that the means to solve common interpersonal problems seen as most effective are shared by normals differing widely in psychological sophistication and educational background (Siegel, Platt, and Spivack, 1973). The suggestion is that the style as well as the content of problem-solving differ in significant ways when one compares individuals who differ in level of social adjustment, that these differences are not explainable in terms of obvious background variables, and that there is much to be learned in the careful study of the relationship between the style and content of interpersonal problem-solving.

Knowledge about the cognitive interpersonal problem-solving of older children, adolescents, and adults has not yet been formulated into a training program and tested. The fact that successful application has taken place with preschool children and that a script for kindergarten children is being tested suggests that it is only a small step to devise such mental health curricula for use throughout the school years. Siegel and Spivack (1973) have described an application of this approach in the individual treatment of chronic schizophrenics, and pilot work is underway to assess its effectiveness. The program is sequenced to teach a series of interpersonal skills through the use of pictures and tape-recorded interpersonal interactions. Platt, Spivack, and Swift (1973) have designed a similar program for groups of young adults and adults who are having adjustment problems. One application of similar principles has proved effective in work with incarcerated drug addicts (Platt, 1973; Platt, Scura, and Hannon, 1973).

Attempts to design problem-solving programs for older children and adults and especially for disturbed groups have raised some challenging questions worthy of study. Should the design of intervention programs for older children and adults follow the same sequence of lessons that has proved successful with young children? Or can different levels and facets of problem-solving be taught at the same time? Also it is necessary to study whether alteration in thinking style is sufficient to alter overt behaviors that have over the years created their own problems and negative influence on thinking style. Does the potential mediating and controlling function of such thinking lack power to alter habitual, maladaptive behaviors in adults? Is it necessary to intervene in both the style and content of problem-solving? It might be argued that in some cases it is necessary to teach someone what to do or say and not merely how to think about interpersonal problems. The approach in the program for young children stresses that the aim is to affect the style and not to tell the child what he should do or say. The goal is to enhance an approach to problem-solving and not the child's storehouse of solutions to specific problems. The research evidence indicates that at all age levels the ability to create problem-solving thought differentiates individuals at different social adjustment levels. Knowing *how* should have greater applicability than learning what to do in a particular instance.

Experience with disturbed adults suggests that often the patient wants to talk about his problem and not the hypothetical one in the program script. This tendency may require a flexible script for older individuals that allows integration of the patient's problems and attempts to deal with them in the training process itself.

Even the limited evidence available suggests that in psychotherapy or counseling attention should focus on how the patient goes about solving a problem. Awareness that one has really been angry at one's spouse and that this has led to an unsatisfactory relationship may not necessarily imply that the patient now knows how to think through the next steps toward resolving his troubles. Some individuals may have perfected such problem-solving skills but are unable to apply them in a certain area of interpersonal conflict. Insight and anxiety reduction may suffice with such patients. Other individuals, because of life-long interpersonal difficulties or chronic disturbances, may never have developed these thinking skills to begin with. For them insight into motive may be insufficient for improved adjustment. Insight may only induce another form of anxiety because the person not only recognizes that he must do something different but also that he is unable to think of what he should do and how to do it.

Despite the numerous unanswered questions about specific applications of this program there are possibilities for immediate application of certain aspects in diverse settings. There is no reason why the dialogues and games cannot be applied in any classroom or therapeutic interaction with children and adults. In essence they define a way of relating to people that focuses on helping them understand and verbalize certain feelings and interactions, encourages them to see and verbalize the numerous possibilities open to them in working with others, and extends their minds both temporally and spatially to encompass those around them.

II

The Training
Program Script

This chapter presents the detailed script the trainer uses to increase the problem-solving ability of four-year-old children. The general outline of the program, the rationale of each game, and general instructions to the trainer have been described in Chapter Three. The program script in this chapter contains the detailed day-by-day description of the program including dialogues, how to apply the games and procedures, stage cues to the trainer regarding techniques of presentation, and the materials used.

It is not necessary to memorize the script. The trainer can put it in her lap and casually read from it while talking to the children, even when presenting the puppet stories. The

138

book can be put on a table or chair when the trainer is pointing to pictures placed on the blackboard. Children's names mentioned in the script should be replaced by the names of children in the group.

As described in Chapter Three the program takes a maximum of twenty minutes per day. Because of illness, too many children absent, holiday preparations, and the like there are days when formal training is not possible. Though the forty-six days in the script total about nine school weeks the program generally takes eleven or twelve weeks to complete.

The day numbers are only a guide and can be adapted to the pace of the group.

Once the trainer begins using the script she may begin to create variations in specific games or problems. But only technique may be changed, not the purpose of the lesson. A teacher may, for example, create a new situation to elicit consequences but in so doing she must not lose sight of the meaning of the lesson and the seven principles of teaching outlined in Chapter Two.

The materials that were developed for the research project may be replaced with similar materials at hand or made by the trainer.

The 2 x 3 foot flannel magnetic board and magnets are obtainable through the Instructo Corporation (Paoli, Pa. 19301). There is no reason why a plain blackboard and some tape (to hold up the pictures) would not work just as well. Artificial flowers and animal trinkets may be obtained from party or novelty shops and dime stores. The alligator (or dragon), whale, duck, (or crow), and finger puppets depicting people may be obtained through Creative Playthings (Princeton, N.J. 08540).

The following pictures are available from the David C. Cook Publishing Company (Elgin, Ill. 60120): My Community, Food and Nutrition, Transportation, Social Development, Helping and Sharing (flannel board). The picture set Big Little Animals is available from M. A. Donohue and Company (Chicago). The two storybooks—*Will I Have A Friend?* by Miriam Cohen (1967) and *The Circus Baby* by Maud and Miska Petersham (1950)—are published by Macmillan.

PREREQUISITE SKILLS

— DAY 1 —

GAME 1: IS

Now we're going to play a game. Are you ready? OK. Watch me very carefully.

Johnny IS a boy. Is Johnny a boy? *Children reply.* Yes, Johnny IS a boy. *Repeat in quick tempo with each child in the group. If a child does not respond, ask him again and shake his hand saying "good" when he does respond. If a child is teasing by responding with the opposite answer, say:* Johnny are you a boy? *If he continues to tease just say:* OK. I know you're teasing me.

If a child still does not respond ask him again. If he responds shake his hand and say: Good! *If not, encourage him just to shake his head to the question "Is Johnny a boy?" Then shake his hand and reinforce. If he still does not respond encourage him to shake his head with you. Say:* Let's shake our heads together. *Shake your head dramatically.*

Now watch me carefully. When I point to someone who is a girl, raise your hand like this. *Teacher raises hand.*

What are we going to do when I point to a girl? *Children reply.* That's right, raise our hand. *Go through motion.*

When I point to a boy, tap your knee like this. *Teacher taps knee.* What are we going to do when I point to a boy? *Children reply.* That's right, tap our knee. *Go through motion.*

OK. Now watch. *Point to a child and call him by name.* Johnny. *Wait for children to tap.* Good, we tapped our knee because Johnny is a boy. *Continue with each child in the group.*

If a child does not join the group ask him again. If he still does not respond encourage him to tap his knee with you. Say: Let's tap our knee together. Good, we are tapping our knee because Johnny IS a boy. *Do not push the child further at this time.*

— DAY 2 —

GAME 2: A-SOME

Remember yesterday when the game was pointing to A boy and to A girl? Well today we are going to point to SOME girls.

OK. Are you ready? Now watch me very carefully.

Johnny and Bobby are SOME boys. Are Johnny and Bobby SOME boys? Yes (*nodding head*), Johnny and Bobby are SOME boys. Peter is A boy. Peter and Ralph are SOME boys. Is Peter A boy or is Peter SOME boys? *Children reply.* Yes, Peter is A boy. *Continue with each child in the group, sometimes in pairs (some) and sometimes one (a) child.*

Now watch me carefully. I am going to point to SOME girls. When I point to SOME girls, raise your hand like this. *Teacher raises hand.* What are we going to do when

I point to SOME girls? *Children respond.* Right, raise our hand like this.

When I point to SOME boys, we will tap our knee like this. *Teacher demonstrates.* What are we going to do when I point to SOME boys? *Children respond.* Right, we're going to tap our knee. *Go through motion again.*

OK. Now watch. *Point to two children and call them by name.* Johnny and Jimmy. *Children respond.* Good, we tapped our knee because Johnny and Jimmy are boys. Sally and Mary. What do we do? *Children respond.* Good, we raised our hand because Sally and Mary are girls. *Switch between pairs of boys and girls in random order.*

If a child does not respond say: Johnny, what do we do when we point to SOME girls? *Encourage him to raise his hand together with you. When he responds say "good" and shake his hand.*

— DAY 3 —

GAME 3:   NOT

Point to a child. Johnny is a boy. Johnny is NOT (*pause*) a girl. Johnny and Jimmy are boys. Johnny and Jimmy are NOT (*pause*) girls.

Is Peter a boy? *Nod head and say:* Yes, Peter is a boy.

Point to girl and ask: Is Sally a boy? *Shake head and say:* No, Sally is NOT (*pause*) a boy.

Sally is not a ———. *Let children respond.*

Sally is a girl.

Sally is not a boy.

Sally is not a ———. *Let children reply.*

Is Sally a boy?

No, Sally is not a boy.

Repeat with each child in the group and then switch to pairs and use of the word "some." Sally and Susie are SOME girls. They are not SOME boys.

Then try to trick. Sally is a boy. Oh, you caught me. Sally is a ———. *Let children respond.*

Encourage nonresponding youngsters to shake their head in the appropriate direction, and shake their hand if they do.

— DAY 4 —

GAME 4 :   FUN WITH NOT

Yesterday we talked about the word NOT. Today we're going to play a game with the word NOT again. Are you ready?

Johnny is a boy. Johnny is NOT a ———. *If the group does not respond say:* Johnny is NOT a piano. Let's have fun. Let's be silly.

Johnny is NOT a ———. Mary is NOT a ———. Good, Mary, Johnny is NOT a (*repeat response*). Peter is NOT a ———. Good, Peter, Johnny is NOT a (*repeat response*).

After three or four children respond to what Johnny is not, proceed to a new child. If a child says "Johnny ain't no ———" or "Johnny is not no ———," do not correct him. Just casually repeat: Johnny is not a ———. *Learning the concept of the negation is more important than correct language usage.*

At the end of the game, after each child in the group has had a turn being the subject of what he is NOT, switch to: Johnny IS a ———. Good. Johnny is a ———. *Repeat with as many children as interest permits.*

— DAY 5 —

GAME 5:   OR, IS-NOT

Today we are going to talk about the word OR.

Am I pointing to Johnny OR (*emphasize and pause*) am I pointing to Jimmy? *Children reply*. Good, I am pointing to Jimmy.

Am I pointing to Sally OR am I pointing to Susie? *Children reply*. Good, I am pointing to Sally.

Have the children close their eyes and give them some party hats or trinkets. Open your eyes. Who is NOT holding a hat? Raise your hand. Who IS holding a hat? Raise your hand.

Kevin, is Sally holding a hat? *Ask individual children who is and who is not holding a hat. If time permits let those who did not get a hat have a chance to hold one and repeat the game.*

— DAY 6 —

GAME 5 (CONTINUED):   OR, AND

Am I pointing to Richard OR am I pointing to Peter? *Children reply*. Good, I am pointing to Richard. I am not pointing to ———. *Continue with a few children, switching between AM and AM NOT and pointing to* ———.

Diane and Barbara, come and stand up front. Is Diane standing up front? Is Barbara standing up front? *Children respond*. Yes, Diane AND Barbara are standing.

Is Carol standing OR is she sitting? *Children respond*. Yes, Carol is sitting. *Continue the game, pointing to a different child. Switch between the following choices: standing or sitting; boy or girl; am I pointing to Tom or to Sam?; two children standing in front, Paul AND Pat; Bobby is NOT standing; Don is NOT sitting; I am NOT pointing to ————.*

If children stand up or walk around without asking, refer to whatever they are doing, such as: Is Johnny walking or sitting? *Do not insist that he sit down; make his actions part of the game.*

— DAY 7 —

GAME 6: SAME-DIFFERENT

Close your eyes. *Give some children hats and some children flowers or trinkets.* OK. Now open your eyes. Some children have flowers and some children have hats.

Everybody who has a hat, hold it up high. See, some of you are holding hats. *Name each child who has a hat.* Now everybody who has a flower hold it up high. See, some of you are holding flowers. *Name each child who has a flower.*

Is a hat DIFFERENT from a flower? *Children reply.* Yes, a hat is DIFFERENT from a flower. A hat is NOT the SAME as a flower. Is a hat the SAME as a flower? *Children reply.* A hat is DIFFERENT from a flower.

Point to a child who is holding a hat. Who is holding something that is the SAME as what (*child with a hat*) is holding? *Children respond.*

Who is holding something that is DIFFERENT from (*same child as before*)? *Repeat with a child holding a flower.*

Johnny, do you have a hat OR do you have a flower? *Child replies.* Yes, Johnny, you have a hat.

Billy (*who has a hat*), do you have a flower? *Child replies.* No, you do NOT have a flower. *Then to the group:* Does Billy have a hat?

Does Sally have a flower AND a hat? *Children respond.* No, Sally does not have a flower and a hat.

What does Sally have? Sally has a ———.

Call on each child and ask him to tell what he has and what he does not have. Yes, Sally has a hat. Sally does NOT have a ———.

Good, Sally does NOT have a flower.

— DAY 8 —

GAME 6 (CONTINUED)

Today we're going to play another game with the words SAME and DIFFERENT. Now watch carefully.

I'm raising my hand. Now I am raising my hand again. I just did the SAME thing. I raised my hand.

Now I'm going to do something DIFFERENT. I'm going to tap my knee. *Tap.* See, tapping my knee (*keep tapping*) is DIFFERENT from raising my hand. *Raise hand.*

Is tapping my knee (*go through motion*) DIFFERENT from raising my hand (*go through motion*)? *Children respond.* Yes, they are DIFFERENT. Tapping my knee is NOT the SAME as raising my hand.

I am tapping my knee. *Go through motion.* Can you all do the SAME thing? *Let children react.* Good, we are all doing the SAME thing.

A nonresponder can be encouraged by saying: Let's do it together. *Dramatize the act emphatically.*

Johnny, can you do something that is NOT the SAME as tapping your knee? *Let child react.* Good, Johnny is (*name his act*). ——— is not the same as tapping our knee. ——— is DIFFERENT from tapping our knee.

Now let's have some more fun with the words SAME and DIFFERENT. Now I'm stamping my foot. *Stamp foot.*

Is stamping my foot the SAME as patting my head? *Children reply.* No, stamping my foot is NOT the SAME as patting my head. It is ———. *Let children say "different." It will probably be necessary to give the choice of same or different, at least at first.* Good, they are DIFFERENT.

OK. Let's play a game doing the SAME things or DIFFERENT things. Now watch me. Let's all do the SAME thing. *Go through three or four different motions such as rolling hands and tapping head, each time repeating:* Let's all do the same thing.

Now let's change the game. Now I'm rolling my hands. Can you do something that is NOT the SAME as rolling my hands, something that is DIFFERENT? *Let children react.* Good, Tanya is shaking her arm. Shaking arms is DIFFERENT from rolling hands. *Repeat as long as interest permits, sometimes asking for something that is the same as what you are doing, sometimes asking for something different.*

Let a child be leader by having him come up to the front and perform a motion. Ask the group to do the same thing as the child leader, then something different.

If a child indicates he does not want to play try to bring him into the game by noting whatever he is doing, such as: Johnny is walking around. That's different from jumping (*or whatever the rest of the group is doing*). *Such an approach might motivate the child to join the game.*

— DAY 9 —

GAME 7: REVIEW

Repeat Games 1 through 6 with pictures, mixing the following word-concepts: "is," "not," "or," "some," "same-

different." Occasionally use the device of tricking. Place pictures on magnetic board or tape to the blackboard. Any pictures of children in action can be used. One pair of pictures should show different children doing the same thing, such as running.

This is a picture of a boy. Is this a picture of a boy? *Group responds.* This is a picture of a boy.

This is NOT a picture of a boy. Is this a picture of a boy? *Group responds.* No, this is NOT a picture of a boy. This IS a picture of a ————.

Is this a picture of a boy OR is this a picture of a girl? *Group responds.* Good, this is a picture of a girl.

Is this boy standing OR is this boy sitting? *Group responds.* Good, this boy is sitting. He is NOT standing.

These are SOME boys. *Point dramatically back and forth to each picture, emphasizing the word "some."*

Are these SOME boys or are these A boy? *Group responds. Again point dramatically back and forth to each boy.* Good, these are some boys.

Is a boy (*point to picture*) the SAME as a girl? *Group responds.* No, a boy is NOT the SAME as a girl. They are ————. *Give choice of same or different if necessary.*

This boy is eating. *Show a different picture.* This boy is ————. Are these boys doing the SAME thing? *Group responds.* No, they are doing something ————. *Give choice of same or different if necessary.*

This boy is running. This boy is running too. Are these boys doing something that is the SAME or are they doing something DIFFERENT? *Group responds.* Yes, they are doing the SAME thing. This boy is running and this boy is running too.

Is this boy running OR is this boy sitting? *Group responds.* Yes, this boy IS sitting.

What is this boy doing? *Group responds.* Yes, he is playing with a ball.

Is this boy who is playing with a ball doing the SAME thing as this boy who is running? *Group responds.* No, they are doing something ————. *Give choice of same or different if necessary.*

Point to a boy who is not eating. Say: This boy is eating. *Wait for group to respond.* Oh, you caught me. He is NOT eating. He is ————.

Point to a boy. Say: This is SOME boys. *Wait for group to respond.* You caught me again. This is A boy.

Point to some boys. Say: This is A boy. *Wait for group to respond.* You really are catching me now. These are ————. *Use choice of a boy or some boys.*

Peter, tell me, who IS here today? *Let Peter name children present.* Robert, who is NOT here today? *If Robert names someone who is present say:* Robert, is Tommy here today? *Let Robert respond.* Tommy is here today? Who is NOT (*pause*) here today?

— DAY 10 —

GAME 8:   IDENTIFYING EMOTIONS

With pictures: This boy is smiling. Is this boy smiling? *Group responds.* Yes (*Nod head*), this boy is smiling.

This boy is NOT smiling. Is this boy smiling? *Group responds.* No, this boy is NOT smiling.

Terrence, point to a picture of a boy who is NOT smiling. Right, this boy is NOT smiling.

Sally, you point to a picture of a girl who is crying. *Switch between pointing to pictures of a boy and a girl, smiling and not smiling, crying and not crying. Let all the children in the group have a turn at pointing.*

GAME 9:   IF-THEN-NOT

IF Billy is a boy, THEN Billy is NOT a girl.
IF it is daytime, THEN it's NOT nighttime.
IF Sally is a girl, THEN Sally is NOT a ————.
IF your name is Susan, THEN you can NOT jump. Can Susan jump? *Group responds.* No, Susan can NOT jump.
IF your name is NOT Susan, then you CAN jump. Can you jump, Rodney? *Rodney responds.*
Now if your name IS Susan, you CAN jump. Can you jump now, Susan? *Susan responds and can be encouraged to jump.*

— DAY 11 —

GAME 10:   HAPPY-SAD, SAME-DIFFERENT

Today we're going to talk about the words SAME and DIFFERENT again. We're also going to talk about some new words. One new word is (*pause*) HAPPY and another new word is (*pause*) SAD.

Use pictures of a laughing child and a crying child. Point to child who is laughing. This child feels happy. *Point to crying child.* This boy feels sad. *Point to laughing child.* How does this child feel? *Group responds. Give choice of happy or sad.* Yes, he feels happy. How does this child feel? *Point to crying child. Group responds.* Yes, he feels sad.

Point to laughing child. IF this child feels happy and (*point to crying child*) this child feels sad, they do NOT feel the SAME way. They feel DIFFERENT ways.

Point to laughing child. Does this child feel the SAME way or a DIFFERENT way from this child? *Point to crying child.* Same or different? *Group replies.* Yes, they have DIFFERENT feelings. They do NOT feel the SAME way.

Point to laughing child. If this child is laughing (*imitate sound*), then is he happy or is he sad? *Group responds.* Yes, this boy (*point*) and this boy (*point*) feel happy. Do they feel the SAME way OR DIFFERENT ways? *Group responds.* Yes, they both feel the SAME way.

— DAY 12 —

GAME 11:   AND, NOT

Today we're going to talk about the word NOT again. We're going to talk about a new word too. The new word is AND.

Use any picture of people in action, such as a boy reading a book and a librarian behind a desk. Let's talk about this boy. He is sitting down. What else can you say about this boy? He is sitting down AND ———. *Repeat what one child says.* Good, Johnny, he is sitting down AND he is (*repeat what the child said*). What else can we say about this boy.

Always repeat what the child says and all responses stated thus far: He is sitting down AND he is reading a book AND ———. *Responses regarding the clothes he is wearing can be elicited, such as "a hat AND a shirt." As a motivating technique raise your arms like an orchestra leader, simultaneously shouting the word "and." Encourage the group to shout the word "and" with you.*

Now listen carefully. This boy is NOT standing. This boy is not ———. Good, Jimmy, this boy is NOT (*repeat child's answer*). He is NOT ———. *Elicit as many responses as possible. Repeat the game with a new picture.*

— DAY 13 —

GAME 12:   HAPPY-SAD AND HOW CAN WE TELL?

Today we're going to talk about how we can tell if someone feels happy or if he feels sad.

A boy can be happy. A boy can be sad. *Show picture of a boy smiling.* Do you think this boy is happy or do you think this boy is sad? *Group responds.* How can you tell? *If the group says he is smiling or laughing follow with:* Yes, he is laughing. We can tell he is laughing by seeing with our ———. *Point to eyes dramatically.*

If this boy (*point*) is crying, is he happy OR is he sad? *Group replies.* IF a boy is sad, THEN he is not ———. *Give choice of happy or sad.*

Is this a penny? How can you tell? You can see with your ———. *Point dramatically to your eyes.*

Hide a pencil behind your back so that it cannot be seen. I am hiding either a pencil in my hand or I am hiding a key in my hand. Do I have a pencil or do I have a key in my hand? You cannot tell because you cannot see it now. *Bring the object into sight.* Now tell me what this is. *Children respond.* How can you tell? You can see it with your ———. *Point to eyes.*

After playing this game with an object the children will understand that seeing is one way to tell what something is. Now repeat the first part of the game using pictures of crying and laughing children.

— DAY 14 —

GAME 13:   MORE HOW CAN WE TELL?

Let's talk about our eyes some more. Show me your eyes. Point to your eyes. We can see with our eyes. What can we do with our eyes? *Group replies.* Yes, we can SEE with our eyes.

Now close your eyes. Keep them closed. Cover your eyes with both hands. Can you see with your eyes now? *Group replies.* No, you CANNOT see with your eyes when they are closed.

Now open your eyes. Can you see with your eyes now? *Group responds.* Yes, you can see with your eyes when they are open. You can see with your eyes when they are NOT closed.

Now let's talk about our ears. Point to your ears. We can HEAR with our ears. What can we do with our ears? *Group replies.* Yes, we can hear with our ears.

Can we SEE with our ears? *Group responds.* No, we CANNOT see with our ears.

What CAN we do with our ears? *Group responds.* Yes, we can hear with our ears. Can we hear with our eyes? *Group responds.* No, we CANNOT hear with our eyes. What can we do with our eyes? *Use choice of see or hear.* Yes, we can SEE with our eyes.

I am laughing. *Demonstrate.* Am I happy OR am I sad? *Group responds.* How can you tell I am happy? *If response is "you're laughing" say:* How can you tell I am laughing? Did you see me with your eyes? *Let children answer.* Did you hear me with your ears? *Let children answer.*

Yes, you can tell two ways. Way number one (*show one finger*) you can tell I'm happy is to see me with your eyes. *Point to eyes.* You can SEE I am laughing. Way number two (*show two fingers*) you can tell I'm happy is that you can HEAR me with your ears. *Point to ears.*

— DAY 15 —

GAME 13 (CONTINUED)

My eyes can ————. *Point to eyes.*
My ears can ————. *Point to ears.*
Do my eyes and my ears do the SAME thing? *Group responds.* Good, my eyes can see. My ears CANNOT ————. *Children reply.*

What can my ears do that my eyes CANNOT do? *Children respond.* Yes, my ears can HEAR. My eyes CANNOT ————. *Children reply.*

Cover your face with a big book or sheet of paper and laugh dramatically. Am I happy OR am I sad? *Children respond.* How can you tell? *Keep book over your face.* If the children say "you're laughing" follow with: How can you tell I am laughing? *If the children do not say they can hear you, follow with:* Can you SEE me? *Let group reply.* No, you CANNOT see me now. Can you HEAR me with your ears? *Let group answer.* Yes, you can HEAR me with your ears. *Take the book away.*

Now we have two (*show two fingers*) ways to find out if someone is happy. One way is to SEE with our eyes. *Point to eyes.* What is one way? To see with our ————. To ———— ———— ———— ————. *Keep repeating slowly until the children say "see with our eyes."*

Way number two is to hear with our ————. Way

number two is to —— —— —— ——. *Keep repeating slowly until the children say "hear with our ears."*

Now we have two ways to tell if someone feels happy or sad. Can anyone think of a third way to find out if I'm happy? *If no new idea is given, end the lesson. If a child offers "ask him" encourage him to ask.*

— DAY 16 —

GAME 14:   FINDING OUT ABOUT INDIVIDUAL PREFERENCE

I'm going to show you some pictures of animals today. We're going to find out what you would choose. We're going to see that SOME of you will choose the SAME animal and SOME of you will choose something DIFFERENT. We will see that sometimes DIFFERENT children choose DIFFERENT things.

Show pictures from the Big Little Animals set. Who can tell us what this is? *Group responds.* Yes, a dog. Who knows what this is? *Group responds.* Yes, a cat.

If you could choose a cat OR a dog to play with—that means you can only choose ONE (*show one finger*)—which one would you choose, Johnny? *If Johnny does not respond verbally encourage him to point to the one he would choose.*

Angie, which one would you choose? *Ask each child in the group. Depending on the choices, continue the conversation using the words "same" and "different."*

Angie and Johnny chose the cat. Did Angie and Johnny choose the SAME thing or something DIFFERENT? *Group responds.* Yes, Angie and Johnny chose the SAME thing.

Steven chose the cat. Tanya chose the dog. Did Steven and Tanya choose the SAME thing or did they choose something DIFFERENT? *Group responds.*

Yes, Tanya chose the dog. Steven chose the cat. They are DIFFERENT. Do you know what? We found out that SOME of you chose the dog and SOME of you chose the cat. Different children choose DIFFERENT things. Is it OK for Tanya to choose something DIFFERENT from what Johnny chose? *Group replies.*

Yes, it's OK for different children to choose different things. Do all of us choose the SAME thing? *Group replies.* No, we do NOT all choose the same thing. We choose ——— things. *Use choice of same or different.*

Show two new animals from the Big Little Animals set. Peter, would this turtle make you happy? Maybe yes and maybe no. How can we find out? *If no answer is given, elicit one in the following way:* Let's ask him. Peter, would a turtle make you happy? What did we just do to find out if the turtle would make Peter happy? *Let group respond.* Yes, we asked him AND we heard him tell us with our ———. *Point to ears.* Robert, come on up here and point to the animal that you would choose. Oh, Robert pointed to the chipmunk. We found out what Robert chose by watching him point. We could see him point with our ———. *Point to eyes.*

We can find out what children would choose in three ways. We can watch them, see them with our ———. *Point to eyes.* That's way number one. Way number two, we can ask them. When they tell us, we have way number three. We can hear what they say with our ———. *Point to ears.*

Repeat the games with as many pairs of animals and as many children as possible.

— DAY 17 —

GAME 14 (CONTINUED)

Repeat Game 14 with pictures from the Transportation set.

— DAY 18 —

GAME 14 (CONTINUED)

Repeat Game 14 with pictures from the My Community set. Interesting choice pairs include the policeman-fireman and beach-park. Besides asking each child what he would choose, encourage the children to ask each other. Kevin, what do you think Robert would choose? *Kevin will probably name something.* Kevin, how can you find out what Robert would choose? *Encourage Kevin to ask Robert. Repeat with other children.*

— DAY 19 —

GAME 15: DO YOU LIKE?

Today we're going to think of ways to make other children feel happy. OK. Are you ready?

Let's think of all the ways we can, you know, all the things we can DO or SAY to make Sally happy. Anybody have an idea? *Let group respond.*

Maybe that would make Sally happy. Maybe that would not make Sally happy. Let's ask her. Let's say together, Sally, would that make you happy? *If Sally answers yes follow with:* That's one way to make Sally happy. Now let's think of a different way to make Sally happy. Way number two. *Group responds. If Sally answers no follow with:* Oh, that idea did not make Sally happy. We'll have to think of something DIFFERENT.

If Sally replied yes to both ideas say: Now we have two ways to make Sally happy: ——— (*repeat first idea*) AND ——— (*repeat second idea*).

Turn to a new child. Johnny, Sally said ice cream

makes her happy. Does ice cream make you happy? *If Johnny says yes follow with:* Ice cream makes Sally happy. Ice cream does not make Johnny happy. Sally and Johnny do not like the SAME thing. They like ———— things. *Use choice of same or different.*

Now we're going to play a game called Do You Like? Asking "do you like?" is one way to find out what makes people happy.

Kenny, do you like to build with blocks? *Let Kenny reply.* Do you like ice cream? *Let Kenny reply.* Do you like to run? *Let Kenny reply. If Kenny says yes to all three follow with:* Kenny likes blocks AND ice cream AND running. Different things make the SAME child happy. Who does NOT like to build with blocks? *If a child responds say:* Janie does not like to build with blocks. Kenny does like to build with blocks. Everybody does NOT like the SAME thing.

Donald, does Peter like dolls? *Donald will probably answer yes or no but will not ask him without guidance.* Can you ask him? *Encourage him to use the phrase "do you like?" If Peter says no follow with:* Ruth, do you like dolls? *If Ruth says yes say:* Peter does not like dolls. Ruth does like dolls. Different children like different things. We have to find out what other people like. *Continue the game as long as interest permits, encouraging the children to ask each other what they like or what makes them happy. Allow the children to get carried away with the phrase "do you like?".*

— DAY 20 —

GAME 16:   EMOTIONAL REACTIONS

Julie, can you show me a happy face? *If Julie does not respond say:* Let's make a happy face together.

Paul, can you show me a SAD face? We know two

ways people can feel. One way is happy. Way number two is sad. There is way number three. MAD. *Demonstrate a happy look, a sad look, and an angry look.*

Mad and angry are the SAME feeling. *Again demonstrate an angry look.*

Let's make up a story. Let's pretend we know that Sandra likes cookies. If Joan let her have a cookie, would that make Sandra happy? *Let children reply.* Yes, that would make Sandra happy.

How might Sandra feel if Joan would NOT let her have a cookie? *Let children reply.* Yes, she might feel sad (mad).

Now let's pretend Sandra had a cookie in her hand and Joan grabbed it from her and ate it. How might that make Sandra feel? *Let children respond.* Maybe that would make Sandra feel MAD (*show expression*) OR SAD (*show expression*). Let's find out. Sandra, if Joan grabbed a cookie from you, how would that make you feel? *Let Sandra reply.* See, we asked her and we found out how she would feel. She told us she would feel (mad) and we heard her tell us with our ———. *Point to ears.*

Now this is just a game. *Give two children a cookie or raisin and tell one child (Steve) to grab a cookie from the other (Paul).*

Ask Paul: How do you feel about that? *Let Paul reply.* OK, Steve, now give the cookie back to Paul. Paul, how do you feel now?

Let's pretend we know that Tommy lost his dog. Tommy, can you look sad? How does Tommy look? *Let group reply.* How would Tommy feel if he found his dog again? *Let group reply.* Yes, he would probably feel happy.

Now let's pretend Peter found that dog and would not give it back to Tommy. How might that make Tommy feel? *Let group respond.* Maybe that would make him feel mad and maybe that would not make him feel mad. How can we find out? *Encourage children to ask.*

Let's pretend it's real cold outside and Sammy does not have any mittens. So he took YOURS. *Point to a child.* Would you feel happy or mad? *Let child reply.*

What would make you feel mad, Jimmy? *If Jimmy does not respond encourage other children to ask him what would make him mad. Other examples that can follow the same dialogue include: not being invited to a birthday party; if someone broke Peter's milk glass; if someone broke his cookie and ate it; if someone scribbled on his painting; if someone gave Judy a puppy.*

— DAY 21 —

GAME 17:   WHY-BECAUSE

Use a picture from the Social Development set: two boys sitting on the floor playing ball. How does this boy feel? *Use choice of happy or sad if necessary. Let group respond.* How can you tell? *If "he is smiling" is given, say:* How can you tell he is smiling? We can ———. *Point to eyes.*

Now we're going to ask a new question. The question is WHY. Now listen. WHY (*pause*) is this boy happy? Because ———. *Group responds.*

The idea of this game is to think of lots of reasons why this boy might be happy. He might be happy because (*repeat first response*) OR ———. Can anybody think of a different because? *Continue until the group runs out of reasons. If a child says he is sad ask him why. He may have a logical thought, such as "the ball might hit him in the eye."*

From now on, if an answer is opposite to what is expected always ask why.

When a child is asked for a different "because," the first child's response should be repeated, followed by: That might be why. Now the idea of the game is to think of lots of becauses. *In this way the first child does not think his answer is incorrect but instead feels part of the game.*

Another useful picture from the Social Development set is that of a girl falling off her bike with a boy standing beside her. How is this girl feeling? *Use choice of happy or sad if necessary.* How can you tell? *If "she is crying" is given ask:* How can you tell she is crying? We can ————. *Point to eyes.*

Why is she sad? *Group responds.*

Why did she fall off her bike? Because ————.

That's one because. Let's think of lots of different becauses.

Do you have a different because, Kevin? *Continue until the group runs out of ideas. Encourage the children to look at the whole picture (including the tree) for ideas.*

What can this boy *(in the picture)* do or say to make her feel happy? *Group responds.*

That's one way, Ralph. Can anybody think of way number two? Let's think of lots of ways to help this girl feel better. *After another child gives an idea say:* Good, now we have way number two. He can *(repeat first idea)* OR he can *(repeat second idea)*. Who has way number three? *Continue until no further ideas are offered.*

— DAY 22 —

GAME 18:   FINDING OUT ABOUT INDIVIDUAL PREFERENCE

Use the picture of a composite of fruits (grapes, watermelons, bananas, apple, orange) from the Food and

Nutrition set. Today we're going to find out what people like again.

Carrie, if you could choose one of the fruits to eat, and only one, which one would you choose? *If no verbal response is given encourage the child to come and point.*

Steven, would you choose the SAME fruit as Carrie chose or would you choose something DIFFERENT? *Ask each child in the group, pointing out that different children like different things.*

Stacie, is there something here that you do NOT like? *Let Stacie reply.* You do NOT like (*repeat Stacie's answer*). Is there anything else you do NOT like? *Continue with the same child to check his knowledge of the negation. Let child reply after each question. Point to each fruit shown in the picture.*

Stacie, do you like apples?

Do you like grapes?

Do you like watermelon?

Do you like bananas?

Robert, can you find out what Michael likes? *If the child says "ask him" say:* Go ahead and ask him. *Encourage children to ask each other what they like.*

Is it OK if Robert likes bananas and Stacie does NOT like bananas? Yes, it is OK for different children to like different things.

— DAY 23 —

GAME 18 (CONTINUED)

Use the picture from the My Community set depicting a child sick in bed. How does this girl feel? *Let group respond. The children will probably say she feels happy. The girl in the picture is smiling. The following dialogue demon-*

strates to the children that different children might feel differently about the same thing.

Who would NOT feel happy to be sick in bed? *To child who answers:* Why do you think this girl might be happy? Because ———. That's one reason she might be happy. Does anyone have a different reason, a different because? *Let the group respond.*

Go back to other pictures from the Food and Nutrition set and repeat the game on finding out about individual preferences. Continue as long as interest permits, the entire lesson not exceeding twenty minutes.

— DAY 24 —

GAME 19:   A STORY

The story "Will I Have a Friend?" is suitable for reviewing concepts to date. After the line in the story "Sarah was telling Margaret a secret. Jim looked at them. Where was his friend?," add the following dialogue: You know, Jimmy really wants a friend. Nobody is playing with him. How does Jim feel now? *Let children respond.* Why do you think he feels sad? *Let children respond.*

— DAY 25 —

GAME 20:   WHAT MIGHT HAPPEN NEXT? (BEGINNING CONSEQUENCES)

Let's make up a story together and I'll help you. Let's pretend Bobby scribbled on Bernard's painting and Bernard did not like that.

Now let's play the What Might Happen Next? game. If Bobby scribbles on Bernard's painting, what might happen next in the story? *Let group respond.*

Yes, that's one thing that MIGHT happen. What else MIGHT happen next? *Continue until group offers nothing new.*

If not already offered ask: How might Bernard feel, happy or mad? *Group replies.* Yes, he might feel mad. Why might Bernard feel mad? Because ———.

Let's make up what might happen next in the story. What might Bernard DO next? Remember, we're pretending that Bobby scribbled on Bernard's painting. *Make scribbling motion. Let group respond.*

That's one thing he might do. If Bobby scribbles on Bernard's painting, Bernard might (*repeat first response*) OR he might ———. Who can think of something else he might do? *Let group respond.*

Repeat second response. That might happen. Now we have two things that might happen. *Repeat both responses.* Can anyone think of a third thing that might happen? *Group responds. When no new responses are offered, switch to:* What might Bernard SAY if Bobby scribbles on his painting? *Continue until no new consequences are given.*

— DAY 26 —

GAME 20 (CONTINUED)

Using any pictures, repeat the game for Day 25, substituting scribbling with "one boy calls the other a crybaby." Referring to the boy who gets called a crybaby, use such questions as "How might he feel?", "What might he DO next?", "What might he say next?"

GAME 21:   ALLIE STORY—PART ONE (EMOTIONAL FEELINGS)

Use alligator and whale hand puppets. The commerical dragon puppet can be used as an alligator. Tell the following story with different voices for Allie the Alligator and the whale. Move each puppet's mouth as it talks.

ALLIE: I am Allie the Alligator. I have no legs. I cannot run and play with the children. I wish I could run and play with the children.

TEACHER (*Sad voice, turning the puppet's head down*): How does Allie the Alligator feel now? (*Group responds.*) Why does he feel sad? Because ————. One day a big whale saw Allie crying.

WHALE: Allie, why are you so sad?

ALLIE: Because I cannot run fast and play with the children.

WHALE: But you can swim. You can swim faster than all the other alligators. All the other alligators want you to play with them. They like you very much.

TEACHER: Allie smiled and laughed. (*Open the puppet's mouth wide.*) How does Allie the Alligator feel now? (*Group replies.*) Yes, he feels happy. How did he feel before? (*Put his head down again. Let group reply.*) See, before he was sad and now he's (*open the puppet's mouth dramatically, pause*) happy. He feels different now. Allie the Alligator swam with the other alligators and he showed them all how to swim very fast. (*Demonstrate swimming motion.*)

— DAY 27 —

GAME 21: ALLIE STORY—PART TWO (HOW CAN I FIND OUT?)

Keep the whale puppet hidden under the table or behind your back.

TEACHER: Here's Allie again. Remember yesterday we found out that Allie LOVES to swim. How did he feel when he was swimming yesterday? (*Use choice of happy or sad if necessary.*) Yes, he felt very happy because he loves to swim. He's a very fast swimmer too.

ALLIE: I've been swimming all morning. This morning some of my friends asked me to swim with them and I said yes. They know I love to swim. (*With Allie on one hand and the whale on the other, bring the whale in slowly from the side.*) Here comes one of my friends, Whipple the Whale. He loves to swim too.

WHIPPLE: Hi, Allie. We sure had fun swimming this morning. We both love to swim, don't we? Let's go swimming again now. That would make me very happy. (*Pull Allie's mouth in so that he looks sad with his head down, and hold a minute.*) What's the matter, Allie, why do you look so sad? I thought it would make you happy if I asked you to swim.

ALLIE: I was happy when we swam this morning. We swam for a long time. I would NOT be happy to swim again today.

WHIPPLE (*turns away from Allie, speaks in a whispering voice*): I guess he doesn't want to play with me. I'll have to think of something so he'll WANT to play with me. Oh, I know what I'll do. (*Turns back to Allie, speaks in a dramatic and enthusiastic voice.*) Allie, if you don't want to swim right now, do you want to play with my new ball?

ALLIE: No, I don't like that game.

WHIPPLE (*puts head down, then turns to Allie and speaks enthusiastically*): Would you like to go find some food to eat?

ALLIE: Not now, I just ate and I'm not hungry.

WHIPPLE: Gee, Allie, I really want to do something with you. What would you like to do now?

ALLIE: I'd like to play hide-and-seek.

WHIPPLE: OK. I'd like that too. I'm glad I ASKED you. I thought maybe you didn't want to play with me today.

ALLIE: Oh, no. I like you. I just didn't want to swim because I wanted to do something different now. Maybe tomorrow we can swim again. Maybe tomorrow I will want to swim again.

WHIPPLE: OK. Let's play hide-and-seek now. (*Hide Allie behind your back and have Whipple find him.*)

TEACHER: They played hide-and-seek for a while and they were very happy. The next day they went swimming again.

ALLIE (*to children*): Do I like to swim SOME of the time? (*Let group reply.*) Do I like to swim ALL of the time? (*Let group reply.*) No, sometimes I like to swim and sometimes I do NOT like to swim. If I swim too much, I might get tired. (*To child.*) Karl, what do you like to do? (*Karl responds.*) Do you (*repeat Karl's response*) ALL of the time or SOME of the time? (*Karl responds.*) I bet you would get tired if you ——— ALL of the time.

Ask different children these questions; then let them have turns playing with the puppets. You can now leave the puppets as play materials in the classroom and help make Allie and Whipple characters in the class.

— DAY 28 —

GAME 22:   REVIEW

Using the remaining pictures from the Transportation, Big Little Animals, and Food and Nutrition sets or any other interesting pictures, repeat Game 18, Day 22. It is particularly important to ask one child to find out what another would choose. Point out individual differences in preference and review the negation by asking a child what he would not choose, then asking him again to determine his consistency of choice.

— DAY 29 —

GAME 23:   MORE WHY-BECAUSE

Using the duck hand puppet, tell the following story with a different voice for Dilly the Duck. Move the puppet's mouth as he talks.

DILLY: I'm Dilly the Duck. I came to play a game with you today. I came to play the Why-Because game. Let me show you how to play. First I'll play with (*name of teacher*). (*Turn Dilly toward you.*) Miss ———, I'm very tired.

TEACHER: Why Dilly?

DILLY: Because I forgot to take my nap. (*Turn Dilly to children.*) Now I'm going to play with you. When I say something, you all ask real loud, WHY? I'll tell you the BECAUSE. Let's try it. I'm very hungry. Now ask why. (*Let children shout "why?"*) Very good. I'm very hungry because I haven't had my lunch. I like going to school. (*Elicit "why" from the children.*) Because the children are my friends. I can't sing today. (*Elicit "why" from the children.*) Because my throat hurts. Now let's change the game. I'm going to ask you WHY and you make up the BECAUSE. Now listen. (*Turn Dilly to teacher. Dilly continues.*) I am going to the store. I am going to walk. I am not going to take the bus. Can you guess why I'm going to walk?

TEACHER: Because it's a nice day out?

DILLY: MAYBE. Can you think of a different BECAUSE?

TEACHER: Because your friend is walking to the store and you want to walk with your friend?

DILLY (*to children*): See, there's more than one BE-CAUSE. Now let's play together. Johnny won't come to my house and play with me today. Why won't Johnny come to my house and play with me today? Does anybody have a BECAUSE? (*Group responds.*) Maybe he won't come BECAUSE (*repeat response*). Does anybody have a different because? (*Continue until group offers no new reasons.*) Let's play this game again. I like birthday parties. Can you guess why I like birthday parties? (*Group responds.*) Very good. Maybe I like birthday parties because (*repeat answer*). Now let's think of a different because. I like birthday parties because ————. (*Continue until group runs out of reasons.*)

TEACHER: Very good. Maybe Dilly likes birthday parties because (*repeat first answer*) OR because (*repeat second answer*) OR because (*repeat third answer*).

DILLY: I see (*child in class*) is NOT here today. Can you guess why ———— is not here today? (*Repeat dialogue, asking for different reasons.*)

— DAY 30 —

GAME 24: FAIRNESS

Today we are going to learn about the word FAIR. I have a raisin here for each of you and I'm going to let each of you take one. *Give each child one raisin.* Now do not eat it yet. We're going to play a game.

It is FAIR for each child to have one raisin. It is NOT fair if someone has two raisins and someone else does not have any raisins.

Is it fair for each child to have one raisin? *Group replies.* Yes, it is FAIR for each child to have one raisin. I only have enough for each of you to have one.

If Johnny takes two raisins (*take a raisin from one child and give it to another*) then Peter will not have any raisins. Is that fair? *Group replies.* No, it is not fair for Johnny to have two and for Peter not to have any.

How might Peter feel if he wants a raisin and does not have any and Johnny has two? *Group responds.* Yes, he might feel sad (mad, not happy).

Why might he feel————? *Let group respond.* Because it is not fair for Johnny to have two raisins and Peter not to have any. Johnny, now let Peter have his raisin back. OK, now you can all eat your raisins.

If two children want to look at a storybook and one keeps it and does not let the other one see it, is that fair? *Group replies.* No, that is not fair. If two children want to look at a storybook, what is fair? *If no response:* What can they do if they want to look at the SAME storybook? *Let children respond.* Is it fair to (*repeat child's response*)? Why is that fair? *Group responds.*

How might William feel if Karl did not let him see the storybook? *Group responds.* Yes, he might feel sad (mad). What can Karl do to make William feel happy again? *Group responds.*

Is it fair for one child to look at a storybook and then keep it so that the next child can NOT see it? *Group responds.* Why is that NOT fair? *Group responds.*

Can you think of things children do that are NOT fair? *Group responds.* If (*repeat an answer*) is NOT fair, what is the fair thing to do? *Group replies.*

— DAY 31 —

GAME 25:   MORE FAIRNESS

Today we're going to play a new game with the word FAIR.

Let's go on a pretend trip to the zoo. We will go in a car. Let's make a car. *Use big blocks or chairs to form a car with enough seats for half the group.* Now the car is only big enough to take SOME of you. It is NOT big enough to take ALL of you. Some of you can go on the first trip, trip number one, and some of you will go on the second trip, trip number two. Let's have (*name half the children in the group*) go on our first pretend trip now. The rest of you will wait because the car is not big enough to take all of you.

All the children over here (*name children*) are going on the trip now. The rest of you will go later. Wait for us here, we'll be back soon.

If you're going on the trip now, raise your hand. *If any child not going on the first trip raises his hand, correct him. If anybody in the first group does not raise his hand, correct him.*

OK. If you're going on the trip now, let's open the door (*go through motion together with the children*), let's all get in (*have the children sit down*), and let's go (*demonstrate by bouncing*). Can we make the sound of a horn? Let's all drive. I see a cow. What do you see, Terry? *Encourage the children to name animals they see on the trip.*

Very good. We had a fun ride, didn't we? Let's open the door and get out. Now we're back.

Now I'm going on another trip with some children. We're going in the SAME car and I can only take some of you. Who should go on the trip? *Let children answer.*

Name a child who did not go on the first trip. Did Julian go on the first trip? *Group replies.* No, Julian did not go on the first trip. *Name a child who did go on the first trip.* Did James go on the first trip? *Group replies.* Yes, James did go on the first trip.

Is it FAIR for Julian to go now? *Group replies.* Why is it fair for him to go now? *Group responds.* Yes, it is fair for him to go now BECAUSE he did NOT go on the first trip.

Is it FAIR for James to go now? Remember, he did go on the first trip. *Group responds.* Why is it NOT FAIR for James to go now? Because ———. Right, it is not fair for James to go now because he went the first time. We have to give all the children a chance to go on a trip. *Name a few more children and ask if it is fair for them to go on the second trip. Name some children who went on the first trip and some who did not. Then go on the trip with the second group.*

PROBLEM-SOLVING SKILLS

This section has twelve problems divided into three parts: alternative solutions, alternative consequences, and solution and consequence pairing. Before each section is an introduction that discusses the goals, techniques for eliciting responses, and suggestions for applications of the techniques to real-life incidents. Between problems are stories and games to maintain interest.

ALTERNATIVE SOLUTIONS

For Problems 1 through 4 the goal is to teach the child to think in terms of alternatives. Using skills he has acquired in preceding lessons he asks the question "What else can I do?" when confronted with a typical interpersonal problem.

To elicit responses, use the following technique. Place a picture on the corner of the board, state the problem, and encourage the children to repeat the problem. Then say: "The idea of this game is to think of lots of different ways (*or ideas*) for (*repeat problem*)." Say: "I'm going to write your ideas on the board. We want to fill up the whole board." Although the youngsters cannot read, this is a useful motivating technique. After the first idea has been given, say: "That's one way. Who's got a different (*new, another*) way? What can —————— do to (*repeat problem*)? After a few ideas have been given count on your fingers: way one (*repeat solution*), way 2 (and so on). Then encourage the group to say *or* in unison and in a rhythmic tone. You can raise your arms like an orchestra leader and in a rhythmic voice say: "Let's all say together (*pause*) OR." After a few more solutions have been given use the same technique with the phrase "what else?" When ideas are no longer offered change your question to: "What can he say to (*repeat problem*)?" Let the group respond. "That's one thing he can say. Can anyone think of something else he can say?" If a youngster jumps the gun and offers a consequence to a solution, recognize it, do not discourage it, then continue asking for solutions. Record solutions and responses if desired.

An enumeration is a variation of the same solution but not a different solution. The most common enumerations are: giving something (give him candy, give him ice cream, give him potato chips); telling someone (tell his daddy, tell his mommy, tell his sister); hurting someone (hit him, kick him, bite him). Let the children enumerate for a while; then classify using the following words: "Giving ice cream and candy and potato chips are all giving something. Can anyone think of an idea that's different from giving something?" Classifying in this manner helps the children distinguish between mere enumerations and solutions that are categorically different.

If a child suggests a form of giving something such as potato chips, use the following approach: "He would have to find out if he would like potato chips. Do all boys like potato chips?" Group replies. "No, all boys do not like potato chips. Maybe he would like potato chips. How could he find out if he likes potato chips?" Group responds. "Yes, he could ASK him. What could he say?" Group responds. "If he would NOT like potato chips, what else could he do?"

If an enumeration such as "give him ice cream" is offered simply say: "He'd have to find out if he likes ice cream." Classify. "Can anybody think of an idea that's different from giving something?"

If a child offers "make him happy," ask: "What can he do or say to make him happy?"

If an idea is relevant to the stated problem it is acceptable, and value judgments are not communicated to the child. "Hit him" is just as relevant as "please." The general dialogue is: "That's one way. Who can think of a different idea? Remember, the idea of the game is to think of lots of ways."

There are, however, some responses that seem irrelevant to the problem as stated. If the solution does not appear relevant always ask: "Why is that a good idea? Tell me a little more about that." Two commonly given solutions are questionable: "cry" and "be good." In Problem 1, for example, child A wants child B to help him put the toys away. An answer of "cry" could be a reaction to B's not helping him or a solution to make the other child feel sorry for him. Whether "cry" is a reaction or a solution should be questioned. The solution "be good" is typical to problems dealing with adult figures. Often "be good" is not a solution; it is just a phrase commonly used by young children. Ask what he means by "be good" and determine its relevance. An explanation such as "look at TV" is not relevant.

— DAY 32 —

PROBLEM 1

Child A wants child B to help him put the toys away. Use any pictures of children playing with toys or the picture of two boys with a box of toys from the Helping and Sharing set.

Let's pretend both these boys were playing with toys and it's time to put them away. A and B were playing with the toys.

Point to boy. This boy wants that boy (*point*) to help him put the toys away. *Have children give names to the boys.*

What does ——— want ——— to do?

——— wants ——— ——— ——— ———.

With children: ——— wants that boy to help him put the toys away.

Now remember, both boys were playing.

Was ——— playing? *Group responds.* Was this one playing? *Group responds.*

Is it fair for ——— to clean up all by himself and not ———? *Group responds.*

No, it is not fair for ——— to clean up and not ———.

Is it fair for (*other boy*) to clean up all by himself and not ———? *Group responds.*

Is it fair for both boys to help clean up? *Group responds.*

Yes, it is fair for both boys to help clean up.

Why is it fair for both boys to help clean up? Because ———.

It is fair for both to clean up because both were playing.

Now let's pretend ——— will not help ——— put the toys away.

What can ——— DO so ——— will help him put the toys away? *Group responds.*

Repeat a child's response and say: That's one way. The idea of this game is to think of lots of ways that ——— can get ——— to help him put the toys away.

I'm going to write all your ideas on the board. Let's fill up the whole board. Who's got a different (new, another) idea (way)?

He could (*repeat way number one*) OR he could ———. Can anybody think of way number two? *Show two fingers. Group responds.*

Good, Sean gave us an idea. *Shake his hand.* That's way number two. Now we have (*repeat ways number one and two, counting on fingers*). He can ——— OR ———. What else can he do? *Write each new idea on the board as the child gives it.*

Repeat solutions given thus far and then say: All together, OR. *With children:* OR.

Can anybody think of way number three? *If not already given, follow with:* What can this boy (*point*) SAY to this boy (*point*) so he'll help him put the toys away? Let's fill up the WHOLE board.

Let's all say together, what else? *With children:* What else?

It is important to classify enumerations. For example: Can you think of an idea that is different from (giving something, hurting someone, telling someone)? *If giving some-*

thing is mentioned ask children how the child in the picture can find out if the other child wants or likes what he suggests. Avoid saying "That's a good idea." The children will evaluate ideas themselves later. It is all right to say: Good, you gave a DIFFERENT idea.

— DAY 33 —

PROBLEM 2

A girl wants her mother to buy her a box of cookies. Use the picture of a girl with her mother in a grocery store from My Community set. Point to girl. This girl wants her mommy (*point*) to buy her a box of cookies.

What does this girl (*point*) want her mommy to do?

With children: This girl wants her mommy to buy her a box of cookies.

What can this girl (*point*) DO so her mommy will buy her a box of cookies? *Group responds.*

Repeat a response. That's one idea. What's the idea of this game? To think of lots of DIFFERENT ideas. She could (*repeat way one, write it on the board*) OR she could ———.

Let's all say together, OR. *With children:* OR.

Can anybody think of a DIFFERENT way? *Let group respond.* Good, Angela gave a new idea. This girl can (*repeat first idea*) OR she can (*repeat second idea*). All together, let's say, what else? *With children:* What else?

If not already given, ask: What can this girl SAY to her mother so she will buy her a box of cookies?

Keep going, repeat responses, and use the words "or" and "what else?" If the group enumerates, classify as described. Be sure to complete the classification. Do not say: Hitting, kicking, biting are all hurting. Can anybody think of something different? *Instead finish the sentence:* Hitting, kicking, biting are all hurting. Can anybody think of something different FROM HURTING? *If the child offers a trade such as "give her cake," ask how the giver can find out if the other person would like cake.*

— DAY 34 —

PROBLEM 3

A girl wants a lady to read her a story. Use the picture of a librarian and a girl looking at a book from the My Community set. Elicit solutions using the same dialogue as for Problem 2.

— DAY 35 —

Read a story. "The Circus Baby" lends itself to the style of the program. In appropriate places in the story ask: How does ——— feel? Why does ——— feel that way? *After the line in the story "Mother elephant decided that her baby must learn to eat properly just as the circus people did," the trainer can add the following dialogue:* Elephants pick up food with their trunks. *Dramatize.* People pick up food with their ———. *Let group reply.* Do elephants and people pick up food the SAME way? *Group replies.* No, they pick up their food in a ——— way. *Use the choice of same or different if necessary.*

After the line in the story "But she was careful not to break anything," add: Why is it a good idea not to break anything? Because ———.

After the line in the story "Then Mr. Clown's stool gave a loud creak and split into many pieces," the following is suggested: How might Mr. and Mrs. Clown feel when they see this? *Group replies.* What might happen next (what might they do or say)? *Group responds.* What could you do if you spilled everything on the floor? *Group responds.*

— DAY 36 —

PROBLEM 4

A child (in a red shirt) wants another child (pointing to book) to sit down so that he can see the picture book. Use the picture of a group of children listening to a story from the Social Development set. Elicit solutions using the same dialogue as for Problem 2.

CONSEQUENTIAL THINKING

For Problems 5 through 8 the goal is to teach the child to think in terms of consequences to an act. Using skills he has acquired in the preceding lessons, he must answer the question "What might happen next if," for example, "I hit him?" Although no value judgments are placed on solutions the goal is to encourage the child to think for himself, weigh the pros and cons of an act, and then decide whether a solution is a good idea.

A relevant consequence is a reaction by a person (B) in direct relationship to an act performed by (A). For example, if A hit B, B might "hit him back," "tell his mommy," "not play with A anymore," "cry," and so forth.

When B reacts to A's act, A may continue a chain of events. For example, if B hits A back (a direct consequence of A's hitting B), A might "throw a block at him and fight." Throwing the block and fighting is a chain reaction to B's hitting A back, not the direct consequence of A's first hitting B.

To elicit responses, use the following technique. Present the problem in the same way as previously. Elicit alternatives in the usual way until one is given that is conducive to naming consequences. Usually "hit," "grab," "ask," and "tell someone" are the easiest solutions for eliciting consequences. Then say: "OK. Let's make up a different kind of story, a story about what might happen next. Pretend the boy (*repeat solution given*). What MIGHT happen next in the story?" Then say: "I'm going to write all the things that MIGHT happen next on this side of the board." Draw a line down the center. "I'm going to put your IDEAS over here (*left of line*) and what might happen next over here (*right of line*)." Consistent recording of solutions on the left side of the blackboard and consequences on the right side helps the child distinguish between solutions and consequences when being questioned. Then say: "Let's think of lots of things that MIGHT happen next if (*repeat same solution*)." In eliciting consequences, avoid using the word *idea* when the children respond because it will confuse the distinction between solutions and consequences.

After the first consequence has been given, follow with: "That's one thing that MIGHT happen if (he hits him)." Emphasize the word *might*. "Can anyone think of something different that might happen if this boy (*point to boy*) (hits) this boy (*point to boy*)? "Now we have two things that might happen. This boy MIGHT (*repeat consequence*) OR he might (*repeat consequence*)."

When thoughts about what might happen next are no longer offered, change the question to: "What might B (*point to B*) DO if A (*point to A*) (hits him)? Point to the character being asked about to avoid confusion. Frequently the children will tell you that B will say "I'm sorry" if A hits him. Point dramatically to B when asking: "What might

B do if A (*point now to A*) hits him?" Such pointing helps distinguish the role played by each character.

If not already offered, the next question can be: "What MIGHT B SAY (*point to B*) if A (*point to A*) (hits) him? He MIGHT SAY————."

If not already offered, ask: "How might B feel if A (hits) him? Give choice of happy, sad, or mad if necessary.

After it is evident that the children will offer no further consequences, ask: "Who thinks (hitting) IS a good idea? Why?" Child responds. "Who thinks (hitting) is NOT a good idea? Why?" Child responds.

Using one solution at a time, elicit all the consequences you can before going to a new solution. Try to pick different solutions, nonforceful as well as forceful, for evaluation each day. Record consequences if desired.

Treat enumerations of consequences as was the case for solutions. That is, repeat the enumerations, classify, and ask for something different from, say, hurting back.

Handle irrelevant answers in the same way as irrelevant solutions.

It is especially important to question the child about who is doing the act. It could determine whether an act is a consequence or a solution. For example, in Problem 5 the boy wants the girl to let him feed the animals. If a child says "grab the food," it is a solution to getting the food if the boy grabs it. If the girl grabs the food, however, then grabbing might be a logical consequence (she might grab it back if it were grabbed from her). If it is not clear which character is performing the act stated, ask: "Who is doing that?" If the act is an apparent solution when you are asking for a consequence, repeat the question: "What might the girl DO or SAY if the boy grabs the food?"

— DAY 37 —

PROBLEM 5

A boy wants a girl to let him feed the animals. Use the picture of a girl in front of a hamster cage from the Social Development set. Elicit solutions in the usual way. This boy (*point*) wants this boy (*point*) to let him feed the animals. *After a solution is given that is conducive to naming consequences, the following dialogue is suggested, using the solution "push her out of the way" for illustration.*

OK. Let's make up a different kind of story, a story about WHAT MIGHT HAPPEN NEXT. Pretend the boy (*repeat solution given*). *Draw a line down the middle and say:* That's something the boy can do. I'm going to put that over here. *Point to the left side of the line and write the response on the board.*

Now listen carefully. This is a new question. If the boy (pushes the girl out of the way) what MIGHT happen next in the story? *Group responds.* OK, Cheryl, the girl MIGHT (push him back). I'm going to write all the things that MIGHT happen next over here. *Point to the right side of the line and write the response on the board.*

Now let's think of lots of things that MIGHT happen next if (the boy pushes her out of the way). *Let group respond.*

Good, Robert told us what MIGHT happen next. *Write his thought on the board to the right side of the line. Point to girl.* The girl MIGHT (push the boy back if he pushes her). *Point to boy.* That's one thing that might happen. The girl might (cry) if he pushes her. *Continue pointing to each character as it is being described. Repeat the whole sentence; that is, "The girl might cry if the boy pushes her,"* not just *"the girl might cry."* Now we have two (*show two fingers*) things that might happen.

When no further thoughts are offered, change the question to: What might this girl (*point to girl*) DO if this boy (pushes her out of the way)? *Let group respond.* OK, Donald, that's one thing she might do. Can anyone think of something different the girl might do if the boy pushes her? *Elicit different things the girl might do.*

If not already offered ask: What MIGHT the girl SAY to the boy if he (pushes her out of the way)? *Let group respond.* She MIGHT say (*repeat response*) OR she might say ————. Can anyone think of something DIFFERENT she might say?

If not already offered ask: How MIGHT the girl feel if the boy pushes her out of the way? Do you think she might feel happy, sad, or mad? *Let group respond.*

When all thoughts have been completed, follow with: MAYBE SOME of us think (pushing her out of the way) IS a good idea. Maybe some of us think (pushing her out of the way) is NOT a good idea.

If you think (pushing her out of the way) IS a good idea, raise your hand. Mary, why is (pushing her out of the way) a good idea? *Let Mary respond.* OK, Mary, MAYBE it IS a good idea because (*repeat Mary's reply*). Tommy, why do you think (pushing her out of the way) is a good idea? *Let Tommy respond.* OK, Tommy, MAYBE that's a good idea because (*repeat Tommy's reply*).

If you think (pushing her out of the way) is NOT a good idea, raise your hand. Tyrone, why do you think that's NOT a good idea? *Let Tyrone reply.* OK, Tyrone, MAYBE that's NOT a good idea because (*repeat Tyrone's reply*). *Continue to ask each child who raises his hand.*

If a consequence seems irrelevant ask: Why might that happen next?

If consequences are enumerated, such as "she'll hit him," "kick him," and so on, classify in the usual way: She MIGHT hurt him if he (pushes her). What else might she do that is different from hurting him?

If there is time, elicit another solution, write it to the left of the line, and repeat the same line of questioning with the new solution. Use nonforceful solutions such as "say please" and " give her candy" as well as forceful ones such as "hit" "snatch" for eliciting consequences.

If a child wants to change his mind about a solution being or not being a good idea, ask: Why do you think ——— now?

— DAY 38 —

PROBLEM 6

A boy wants a teacher to look at his painting too. Use the picture of a girl and a teacher putting up a painting and a boy holding a painting in front of him from the Social Development set. Elicit consequences using the same dialogue as for Problem 5.

— DAY 39 —

SIMULATED REAL-LIFE PROBLEM

The purpose of this day's lesson is to review many previously learned concepts and to introduce an action game to break up the flow of repeated picture problems. *Give each child a different animal (or other) trinket.* Johnny, what animal do you have? *Ask each child the name of the trinket he is holding.* Brian, would you like to have an animal that someone else has? *If Brian says yes follow with:* Can you think of something you can do or say so ———— will let you have the ————? *If Brian does not succeed say:* Oh, Brian, can you think of a DIFFERENT idea? *Let each child in the group have a chance to obtain an animal that someone else has. If the child's idea is successful follow with:* How does that make YOU feel? *Let the child respond.*

If grabbing or hitting occurs ask: How does that make him feel? *Let child respond.* What might happen next (what might he do or say if you grab that from him)? *Let child respond.* Can you think of a different idea so he will not (be mad, grab it back)?

After each child ends up with the trinket he likes, pick an animal that one child is holding (such as a bear) and say: Who is NOT holding a bear? *If the child holding the bear raises his hand say:* Now listen carefully. Who is NOT holding a bear? *Repeat the questioning, sometimes asking who IS holding a* ———— *and sometimes asking who is NOT holding a* ————.

— DAY 40 —

PROBLEM 7

A child wants his brother to stop breaking his toys. Use any appropriate pictures. Elicit consequences as for Problem 5.

— DAY 41 —

PROBLEM 8

A boy wants his mother to buy him a new puzzle. Use any appropriate pictures of a boy and a woman. If necessary

*draw a puzzle on the board or use a real puzzle from the
classroom. Elicit consequences as for Problem 5.*

— DAY 42 —

PUPPET STORY: REVIEW

The purpose of this lesson is to review earlier concepts through finger puppets. *Use finger puppets of a boy
and a girl.*

BROTHER: (*Make crying sound.*)

SISTER: I wonder why my brother is so sad. (*Turn girl
puppet toward boy puppet.*) Why are you so sad?

BROTHER: How do you know I'm sad? How can you tell?

SISTER: I can see with my eyes that you're crying.

BROTHER: I'm going to put my hands over your eyes.
(*Hold the boy puppet so that he is covering the girl's
eyes.*)

BROTHER: Now you can't see me crying.

SISTER: I can still tell you're sad.

BROTHER: How? (*Crying.*)

SISTER: I can hear you with my ears.

SISTER (*aside*): I wonder why he's so sad. (*To children.*)
How can I find out? (*Let children respond.*)

SISTER: I'll ASK him. Let's ask him together. Why are
you so sad? (*Have children repeat after you.*) Why are
you so sad?

BROTHER: Why do you think I'm so sad?

SISTER: Because you cannot go out and play?

BROTHER: No! (*Pause.*) That's not why I'm so sad.

SISTER (*to children*): Does anybody know why he is so
sad? MAYBE because ———. (*Children respond.*)
Maybe because (*repeat response*) OR who has a different because? (*Children respond.*)

SISTER: I think I know. You want to go to the zoo and no one will take you. Going to the zoo would make you happy, right?

BROTHER: No!

SISTER: No? Going to the zoo would make me happy. I thought that would make you happy too.

BROTHER: I do like the zoo. But I went to the zoo already today. I do NOT want to go to the zoo again now.

SISTER: Oh, I did not know you just went to the zoo. Would going for a walk make you happy?

BROTHER: No! I do NOT like to walk.

SISTER: Walking makes ME happy. I thought walking would make you happy too.

BROTHER: Different people like different things. You like to walk. I do NOT like to walk.

SISTER (*to children*): Do you have any ideas? What might make my brother happy? (*Encourage the responding child to ask the brother puppet if his idea would make him happy.*) Can you ASK him?

Have the brother puppet agree sometimes and disagree sometimes with the children's suggestions. For an inhibited child have the brother agree. If the brother is going to disagree with a suggestion such as candy, follow with the brother saying: Do you like candy, Sally? *Let Sally reply.* Does candy make you happy, Sally? *Let Sally reply.* Candy makes YOU happy, Sally. Candy does NOT make me happy.

SISTER: Can anybody think of something different that might make my brother happy? (*Let child respond.*) Can you ask him? (*Encourage the child to ask the brother puppet. If the brother is going to agree with a suggestion such as going to the store, follow with the brother.*)

BROTHER: Do you like to (go to the store) Robin? (*Let*

Robin respond.) You like to go to the store and I like to go to the store too. Yes, going to the store does make me happy.

SISTER: Who has another idea? (*Let group respond. Encourage the child who responds to ask the brother puppet if his idea would make him happy. After several more ideas have been offered, have the brother agree to several of them and continue.*)

BROTHER: Yes (*repeat child's suggestions*), jumping makes me very happy AND apples AND swimming. See. More than one thing makes me happy. You asked me and you found out what makes me happy and also, by asking, you found out what does not make me happy. Now that you made me happy, I would like to make you happy. Would you like to play with me?

Let each child have a turn playing with the puppets. If more than the two finger puppets are available, distribute them for the children to play with.

Solutions and Consequences Pairing

For Problems 9 through 12 the goal is to teach the child to think of a solution and then think immediately of its consequence. Ultimately it is hoped that the child will learn to think of a solution, weigh its pros and cons, and then decide which alternative is most appropriate before taking action.

Place the picture in the upper left-hand corner of the board and present the problem. You can now use the word *problem* with the children. The problem today is ———. Have the children repeat the problem as usual. Then draw a line in the middle of the board. Say: "Today we're going to play our game in a new way. I'm going to ask you for one idea. I'm going to write it over here." Point dramatically to to the left side of the line. "After we have an idea, I'm going to ask you about what might happen next. I'm going to put what might happen next over here." Point dramatically to the right side of the line. This visual distinction will help clarify the difference between a solution and a consequence.

After eliciting one solution ask immediately what might happen next as a consequence to that solution. To elicit consequences ask one of the following questions until one consequence is given: "What might happen next?" "What might B do if A ———?" "What might B say if A ———?" "How might B feel if A ———?"

Ask for one consequence only. Then go to the second solution. After one new solution has been given switch to eliciting a consequence. Occasionally call on one child at a time and ask: "What's your idea, Shelly?" Let Shelly respond. "Shelly, if (repeat Shelly's response) what might happen next?" Occasionally follow with: "Is that a good idea?" Let the child respond. "Why is (is that not) a good idea?" Treat enumerations, acceptable and questionable responses, and chaining as for alternative solutions and alternative consequences.

— DAY 43 —

PROBLEM 9

A girl on a bike wants a boy on a wagon to get out of her way. Use the picture of a girl and boy riding in a playground from the My Community set.

The problem today is: This girl on the bike (*point*) wants this boy (*point*) on the wagon to get out of her way.

What is the problem? What does the girl want the boy to do? *Children repeat the problem.*

Today we're going to play our game in a new way. I'm going to ask you for one idea. I'm going to write it over here. *Draw a line down the middle of the board and point dramatically to the left side of the line.*

OK. Who has an idea of what this girl (*point*) can do so this (*point*) boy will get out of the way?

After one solution has been offered say: OK. Now listen carefully. This is a hard question. If (*repeat the solution*) then what MIGHT happen next? *If a consequence is not offered follow with the remaining questions, such as:* What might B do (say) if ———? *As soon as one consequence is offered say:* OK, that might happen. I'm going to put all the things that might happen next over here. *Point dramatically to the right side of the line.*

Now listen again. I'm back to this side of the board (*point to the left side of the line*). Now we need an IDEA again, something the girl can DO or SAY so the boy will get out of the way. Ralph, what's your idea? *Let Ralph respond.* OK, if the girl (*point to the girl and repeat Ralph's idea*), then what might happen next? What can I write on this side of the board? *Point to the right side of the line.*

Repeat this line of questioning, always alternating solution and consequence, intermittently asking: Is that a good idea? Why is that a good idea? *Such questions should be asked for nonforceful ("ask him") as well as forceful ("hit him") solutions.*

— DAY 44 —

PROBLEM 10

A girl on top of a slide wants a boy at the bottom to get off so that she can slide down. Use the picture of children in a playground from the Social Development set. Follow the dialogue for Problem 9.

— DAY 45 —

PROBLEM 11

A boy wants a man to give him a ride on the firetruck. Use the picture of a boy, a dog, and two firemen from the My Community set. Follow the dialogue for Problem 9.

— DAY 46 —

PROBLEM 12

One child wants another to come to his house and play. Any pictures of children are suitable. Follow the dialogue for Problem 9.

At this point the formal preschool script ends. But interacting with the children on the basis of this approach should not end here. As described in Chapters Five and Six there are ways to use the program informally throughout the day.

12

Evaluation
Measures

Although studies have demonstrated that use of the program script and style alters both cognitive and behavioral adjustment in predicted directions, users of the program and its approach may wish to evaluate it in their own setting. This chapter describes the final measures developed to evaluate the program during its research phase. They may be applied before and after the program to assess the extent of its success. There is no reason to doubt that the program may enhance behavioral adjustment as measured by other instruments, but the measures described here have proved sensitive in assessing program effectiveness.

Cognitive Measures of Problem-Solving

The two measures of cognitive problem-solving ability most intimately related to behavioral adjustment measure the child's

192

ability to think of alternative solutions and his ability to think of alternative consequences to solutions. The ability to think of alternative solutions is measured by the PIPS test. Consequential thinking ability is measured by the What Happens Next? game. Each test is administered individually to the child and takes between twenty and twenty-five minutes to complete. We suggest that they be administered at different sittings to avoid exceeding the child's interest span. Experience indicates that it is best to administer them in a separate room as free of distractions as possible. Usually the children are eager to participate once the procedures have been presented as games and the obvious need for rapport has been taken into consideration. It is a help, in presenting each interpersonal test situation, to be dramatic: "Oh-oh! You know what Billy did? He broke his mother's favorite flowerpot and he is afraid. . . ." In both measures there are standard means of probing for responses to questions. These means should be followed so that each child is tested following standard procedures.

The PIPS test has two parts. The first presents a series of problem situations between peers in which one child wants to play with a toy another child is playing with. In the second part the child has done something to make his mother angry. The child being tested is asked what the child in the story can do so that he can have a chance to play with the toy or so that his mother will not be angry. For each situation, pictures are used to depict the child, the mother, and the toy. Any pictures of age-relevant children the same sex as the child being tested can be used, as well as typical objects or toys that are attractive to children this age. Toys likely to invite cooperative play (a wagon, a ball) have been avoided so that the obvious solution of playing together would not be suggested. Nineteen colored pictures of boys, nineteen of girls, fifteen of toys, and seven of mothers are necessary to test a wide variety of children. The characters are presented on 5 x 8 cards and the toys on 3 x 5 cards. Experience indicates that interest wanes unless new pictures are introduced to depict each new problem. In each instance the characters are given different names to maintain interest and variety. The test is presented with the following introduction: "We want to know how children think about things. I've got some pictures and I'm going to tell you some stories about children. I'm going to tell you the first part of the story, and I want you to make up the rest of the story. I want you to tell me what you think the child could do in the story. Pretend all the children are (age of child being tested). OK?"

If the child is able to give different solutions to the basic peer stories, new situations can be added by introducing a new and desirable object (bike, teddy bear, telephone, and so forth). The seven basic peer stories follow.

(1) "Here's (child A in the picture) and here's (child B). A is playing with this truck and he has been playing with it for a long time. Now B wants a chance to play with the truck but A keeps on playing with it. Who's been playing with the truck for a long time? You can point. That's right, A. (Point to A.) Who wants to play with it? That's right, B. What can B do so he can have a chance to play with the truck?" (If there is no new relevant response: "What can B say . . . ?")

(2) "Now let's pretend that C has been playing with the shovel all morning and D would like to have a chance to play with it. C keeps on playing with it. Who's been playing with the shovel all morning? Right, C. Who wants a chance to play with it? Right, D. What can D do so he can have a chance to play with the shovel?" (If necessary: "What can D say . . . ?")

(3) "Now let's say it's this way. E has been out in the yard for the whole play period, playing with this kite. F thinks he would like to play with the kite. Who's been playing with the kite for the whole period? Right, E. Who wants to play with the kite now? Yes, F. What can F do so he can get a chance to fly the kite?" (If necessary: "What can F say . . . ?")

(4) "Today G wants to use the swing but H is already on it. Who is already on the swing? Right, H. Who wants a chance on the swing? That's right, G. What can G do so he can have a chance on the swing?" (If necessary: "What can G say . . . ?")

(5) "One day J was playing with this drum and he was playing with it for a long time. K wanted to play with it. Who has been playing with the drum? Right, J. Who wants to play with it? Right, K. What can K do so he can get to play with the drum?" (If necessary: "What can K say . . . ?")

(6) "L has been playing with this boat for a long time and now M wants to play with it. Who's been playing with this boat for

a long time? Yes, L. Who wants to play with it? Right, M. What can M do so he can get to play with the boat?" (If necessary: "What can M say . . . ?")

(7) "M has had the top all morning and N wants to have a chance with it. Who's been playing with this top all morning? Right, M. Who wants to play with it? Yes, N. What can N do so he can get to play with the top?" (If necessary: "What can N say . . . ?")

After the series of peer problem situations the basic series of five problems is presented in which the story child has done something to make his mother angry with him. In each situation the child being tested is asked what the story child can do or say so that his mother will not be angry with him. The five basic mother problems follow.

(1) "A broke his mother's favorite flowerpot and he is afraid his mother will be mad at him. What can A do or say so his mother will not be mad?"

(2) "Now let's pretend that B scratched his mother's wooden table and made a big scratch or mark on it. His mother might be mad at him. What can B do or say so his mother won't be mad at him?"

(3) "Now let's say it's this way. C burned a hole in his mother's best dress and he is afraid his mother will be mad at him. What can C do or say so his mother won't be mad at him?"

(4) "One day D tore some pages in his mother's favorite book and he was afraid his mother would be mad. What can D do or say so his mother won't be mad?"

(5) "E was playing ball and the ball hit a window and the window broke and he knows his mother will be mad at him. What can E do or say so his mother won't be mad?"

It is important to follow a standard method of inquiry and dialogue with the child. After the child's first response to the first picture the tester should say: "OK! That's one idea. That's one thing he might do. Now the idea of this game is to think of lots of different things the little boys can do."

If the child gives a different solution to each basic story the procedure can be continued with a broken dish, ashtray, and so forth.

If the child repeats in a new situation the same solution he previously offered, say: "That's what Billy (name of boy in previous situation) thought of doing. Can you think of something different that Johnny can do? The idea is to think of all the *different* things the little boys might do to get to play with toys."

If the child offers essentially the same response (enumeration) as previously (hit him, whack him, punch him; or give him candy, give him gum, give him a cookie), say: "That's kind of like what Billy thought of doing before. Hitting and whacking are kind of alike. They are both hurting. Can you think of something *different* from hurting he could do or say?"

Three such probes to encourage a different solution are to be made for each peer problem and each mother problem. If all seven peer situations elicit different solutions, testing continues with the remaining toys. With the remaining toys, however, testing stops after the first toy for which no new solution is given, using the same probing. The same procedure is to be followed with the mother problem situations. Untrained children rarely go beyond the basic series.

The total PIPS score is the number of different solutions given by the child to the peer and mother problems. The total score combines the peer and mother problem scores because of the significant correlation between the two (see Shure, Spivack, and Jaeger, 1971). The average preschool child obtains a score of 5 before training. The main issue in scoring is to separate solutions that are really different from those that are mere enumerations or repetitions of previous solutions in slightly different language. Examples of enumerations for the peer problem are: "Tell his mother," "Tell his father," "Tell his brother." These are all forms of the same solution: asking for some authority to intervene. In the mother problem the same situation occurs when the child says "Give Mommy a cookie" and then "Give Mommy cake." An example of a mere repetition is: "Ask him for it," "Say 'Can I have it?' ", and "Ask if I can hold it."

If the child says something irrelevant to a story the tester merely repeats the story to steer the child back to the problem. Some children solve the situation by finding a substitute for what they want: the child says he will play with something else if he cannot have the kite. In such cases the tester has only to direct the child back to the issue: "Yes, he could do that. But our game is to tell what Billy might do or say so he can get a chance to play with the kite." In all such instances during the basic series of stories, only three such probes or bringing the child back to the problem are carried out before moving on to the next problem. There are numerous unusual (if not ingenious) solutions that youngsters offer, all of which can be scored if they are relevant. The most typical, relevant, and easily scored solutions follow.

Typical peer problem solutions include: share it or take turns, ask or beg, say please, wait for it, trade ("If you give me it, I'll give you my candy."), loan ("I'll give it right back; I'll keep it for a little while."), force or grab ("Hit him," "Beat on him"), command ("Give it to me!"), and invoke authority ("Tell the teacher.").

Typical mother problem solutions include: replace it ("Buy a new one."), repair it ("Glue the pot together."), clean it up, apologize or tell the truth, invoke authority ("Tell Daddy to help me."), say "Don't be mad," hide, hide it, blame another ("Sister did it."), and manipulate affect ("Hug her.").

The What Happens Next? game to measure consequential thinking is presented to the child in the following fashion: "We're going to play the What Happens Next? game. We're going to tell stories together. I'm going to begin this story and I want you to tell me what happens next. Here is the first story."

Each brief story ends with a child grabbing a toy away from another child or having done something without asking permission from an adult. Then the child is asked: "What might happen next in the story?" There are five basic peer stories and five basic stories involving an adult. The toys grabbed are depicted in color on 2 x 3 cards. The children and adults are represented by 3-inch (child) and 3 1/2-inch (adult) stick figures painted different colors, all having round, flat faces with neutral expressions. As with the PIPS test the characters and cards are shown to the child as the stories are presented, for interest's sake and to clarify who said or did what to whom. The child stick figures are given different names, the same sex as the child being tested. The basic question is always the same— "What might happen next?"—and the same probing technique is used as with the PIPS. If the child seems confused the most useful probe is "What might A *do* if B snatches that truck?" and then (if needed) "What might A *say* if B snatches that truck?" Here are the five basic peer stories used in the What Happens Next? game.

(1) "A had a truck and he was playing with it. B wanted to play with that truck. So B grabbed—you know, snatched—that truck. Tell me what happens next."

(2) "Now we're going to make up a new story, different from the first one. OK? A was playing with this shovel in the sandbox. B wanted to play with the shovel. So B grabbed it—snatched it from him. Tell me what happens next."

(3) "Now we're going to tell another different story. Can you make up a third ending? A was playing with this drum in his yard. B wants to play with this drum. So B grabbed it—snatched it from him. Tell me what happens next."

(4) "Now let's see if you can think of an even different new ending. A was playing with this boat. B wanted to play with this boat. So B grabbed it—snatched it from him. You finish the story."

(5) "Let's have another new ending. A was playing with this spinning top. B wanted a chance to play with it. So B grabbed it—snatched it from him. You finish the story. Tell me what happens next."

If five different consequences are given, the procedure is continued with other toys and probes following the PIPS procedure. The child is then presented with the following five adult stories.

(1) "Here's A and this is Mrs. Smith. A saw Mrs. Smith's little poodle dog on her porch and took it for a walk. But A did not ask Mrs. Smith if he could take it. What might happen next in the story?"

(2) "Here's B and here's Mrs. Brown. B took Mrs. Brown's flashlight and did not ask her if he could use it. What might happen next in the story?"

(3) "Here's C and this is Mrs. Hill. C was in her house and saw a small wooden statue on the table. He took it home to show someone but he didn't ask Mrs. Hill if he could take it. What might happen next in the story?"

(4) "Here's D and this is Mrs. Green. D saw Mrs Green's little terrier dog outside her house and took it for a walk. But D did not ask Mrs Green if he could take it. What might happen next in the story?"

(5) "Here's E and this is Mrs. Scott. E was at her house and saw her beautiful new tablecloth and took it to use that night. But he didn't tell Mrs. Scott he was going to take it. What might happen next in the story?"

If the child gives five different consequences to the basic stories the following three stories are used as long as the child gives different consequences.

(6) "Here's F and here's Mrs. Peters. F was in her house and saw a small fan in the corner of the floor and decided he would like to use it for awhile. But he didn't tell Mrs. Peters he was going to use it. What might happen next in the story?"

(7) "Here's G and this is Mrs. Wright. G took Mrs. Wright's umbrella one day but he did not tell her he was going to use it. What might happen next in the story?"

(8) "Here's H and this is Mrs. Wilson. H saw Mrs. Wilson's cat walking in front of her house and decided to take it for a walk. But he did not tell her he was going to take it for a walk. What might might happen next in the story?"

If B is the child who grabs and A is the child whose toy is grabbed away, typical scoreable consequences to the peer-grab stories are: A retaliates by hitting back or harming B in a similar physical way, A gets some authority figure to intervene in his behalf, A will be sad or A will cry, A will say "give it back" or "give it to me" or some other form of demanding the toy be returned, A says he will not be B's friend anymore, A says he did not like that toy anyway, A breaks the toy in anger so that neither can use it, A breaks the toy in the act of grabbing it back, A threatens B ("If you don't give it back I'll tell your mother."), A gets angry at B, A and B get into a fight, A grabs the toy back.

Typical scoreable consequences to the adult-permission stories include: all forms of physical punishment (the child is spanked, hit, or slapped), nonphysical punishment (the child is sent to bed, the child is told he is bad, the adult tells his mother or father what he did, *all scored as separate consequences*), the adult yells at the child (this may be revealed in the child's tone of voice when he tells what the adult says, as well as in the words themselves), the adult gets mad, the adult is sad ("Mrs. Wilson cries."), the child is sad (and this feeling is stated in the story), the adult hides the dog, the object hurts the child (dog bites, fan cuts), the object or dog is lost or hurt (*all scored separately*).

Children at times respond to what might happen next with a solution rather than a consequence: "A will say he won't take the dog again." Here the child is solving the problem of how to avoid the adult's anger and not the immediate consequence of having taken the dog without permission. When the response is irrelevant or repetitious the tester must redirect the child with appropriate probes to the story and the question of what might happen next. If more than one scoreable consequence is given spontaneously to a story, all are included in the child's total score. The average preschool child obtains a total score of 5 on the What Happens Next? game; the total score is the number of different solutions given to both parts of the test.

Behavorial Measures of Adjustment

The overall behavioral adjustment of the child has been assessed through ratings made by teachers and day-care center aides based on their experience with the child in the setting. The scales described in this section derive from extensive early work in scale development (see Spivack and Spotts, 1966a, 1966b) and were refined during the research phase described in Chapter One.

The form to be used in making the overall adjustment ratings contains seven items, all requiring the rater to think in terms of the overt behavior displayed by the child. Early research with scales indicates that these seven items define three behavioral factors. Items 1 and 7 define the extent to which the child has difficulty delaying gratification; Items 2, 3, and 6 tap proneness to emotional upset; and Items 4 and 5 measure social aggressiveness. These three behavioral dimensions correlate significantly with one another although they are not identical in meaning.

A score on each dimension or combined total scores may be used to assess change as a function of the program, depending on the ratings of a child. A child may be considered abnormally inhibited if he receives a rating of 1 or 2 on Items 1 and 7, 4 and 5, or 2, 3, and 6. Thus inhibition may be said to define a problem for the child when he exhibits excessive control of behavior or feelings or is too timid to display even normal amounts of aggressiveness. Impulsiveness as a problem is measured by combining scores on all seven items. A child may be considered as exhibiting minor problems of impulsiveness when his total score is in the range of 38 to 42. As scores increase into the 50s severe impulsiveness is revealed; scores in the high 50s signify a behavioral disturbance of major proportions. Children who are classified as neither overly inhibited or impulsive may be considered as behaviorally adjusted.

To begin rating overall behavioral adjustment think of the average four- or five-year old. Indicate how this child compares with the average child his age and sex. For each behavioral item (considered separately) rate the child as follows.

If the child displays the behavior being rated less often than he should because he is too inhibited, timid, or fearful, rate the child 1 or 2. A rating of 1 reflects more inhibition than 2.

If the child displays the behavior being rated less often than the average child because his adjustment or maturity is better than average, rate the child 3 or 4. A rating of 4 describes well-adjusted behavior; a rating of 3 shows best-adjusted behavior.

If the child displays the behavior being rated about as often as the average child of the same age and sex, rate the child 5.

If the child displays the behavior being rated more often than the average child, rate the child from 6 (somewhat more) to 9 (much more). High scores reflect great amounts of such negative behaviors as impatience, overemotionality, and aggression.

Using the rating system described, the child is rated on the following seven behavioral characteristics.

With this range of scores from 1 to 9 (from inhibition to aggression), the following seven behavioral characteristics are rated. Item 1: peristent and nagging (persist when told he cannot have something; nags, demands, repeatedly asks for something). Item 2: easily upset by peers (when teased or pushed). Item 3: easily upset by adults (gets upset or overemotional if things do not go his way). Item 4: dominant (bosses, threatens, dominates other children). Item 5: physically aggressive (hits, bites, scratches, pushes during free play with peers). Item 6: prone to emotional upset (reacts with immediate anger or upset if another child interferes with his play or takes something that is his). Item 7: impatient (unable to wait or share, grabs toys, unable to take turns—a high score shows more grabbing and less patience).

Four other behavioral items have been shown to relate significantly to problem-solving skills (independent of IQ) and to improve significantly as a function of the training program: the child functions autonomously (completes activities by himself; overcomes obstacles by himself), the child shows initiative, the child shows concern for or offers help to a child in distress, the child is liked by his peers (they seek him out and enjoy being with him). The child can be rated on these four items with a nine-point scale ranging from 1 (very little or no display) through 5 (average) to 9 (much more than average).

Bibliography

ASHER, J. J. "Toward a Neo-Field Theory of Problem Solving." *Journal of General Psychology,* 1963, *68,* 3–8.

BEREITER, C., and ENGLEMANN, S. *Teaching Disadvantaged Children in the Preschool.* Englewood Cliffs, N.J.: Prentice-Hall, 1966.

BIBER, B., and LEWIS, C. "An Experimental Study of What Young School Children Expect from Their Teachers." *Genetic Psychology Monographs,* 1949, *40,* 3–97.

BRONFENBRENNER, U. "Is Early Prevention Effective? Report and Reaction." Presented at Society for Research in Child Development, Philadelphia, 1973.

CALDWELL, B. M. "What is the Optimal Learning Environment for the Young Child?" *American Journal of Orthopsychiatry,* 1967, *37,* 8–22.

CHILMAN, C. S. *Growing Up Poor.* Publication 13. Washington, D.C.: Welfare Administration, 1966.

COATES, G. D., ALLUISI, E. A., and MORGAN, B. B. "Trends in Problem Solving Research: Twelve Recently Described Tasks." *Perceptual and Motor Skills,* 1971, *33,* 495–505.

COHEN, M. *Will I Have a Friend?* New York: Macmillan, 1967.

DAVIS, G. "Current Status of Research and Theory in Human Problem Solving." *Psychological Bulletin,* 1966, *66,* 36–54.

203

DUNCAN, C. P. "Recent Research on Human Problem-Solving." *Psychological Bulletin*, 1959, *56*, 397–429.

D'ZURILLA, T. J., and GOLDFRIED, M. R. "Problem-Solving and Behavior Modification." *Journal of Abnormal Psychology*, 1971, *78*, 107–126.

FEFFER, M. "Developmental Analysis of Interpersonal Behavior." *Psychological Review*, 1970, *77*, 197–214.

FEIN, G. G., and CLARKE-STEWART, A. *Day Care in Context*. New York: Wiley, 1973.

GIEBINK, J. W., STOVER, D. S., and FAHL, M. A. "Teaching Adaptive Responses to Frustration to Emotionally Disturbed Boys." *Journal of Consulting and Clinical Psychology*, 1968, *32*, 366–368.

GOLDFRIED, M. R., and D'ZURILLA, T. J. "A Behavioral-Analytic Model for Assessing Competence." pp. 151–196 in C. D. Spielberger (Ed.), *Current Topics in Clinical and Community Psychology*. (vol. I) New York: Academic, 1969.

GRAY, S., and MILLER, J. O. "Early Experience in Relation to Cognitive Development." *Review of Educational Research*, 1967, *37*, 475–493.

GROTBERG, E. (Ed.) *Critical Issues in Research Related to Disadvantaged Children*. Princeton: Educational Testing Service, 1969.

HARTMANN, H. *Essays on Ego Psychology*. New York: International Universities Press, 1964.

HERTZIG, M. E., BIRCH, H. G., THOMAS, A., and MENDEZ, O. A. "Class and Ethnic Differences in the Responsiveness of Preschool Children to Cognitive Demands." *Society for Research in Child Development Monographs*, 1968, *33*, 1.

HESS, R. D., and SHIPMAN, V. *Cognitive Elements in Maternal Behavior*. Mimeographed, Research Grant 34. Washington, D.C.: Children's Bureau, Department of Health, Education, and Welfare, 1966.

HOLZWORTH, W. A. *Effects of Selective Reinforcement Therapy in a Miniature Situation in Nursery School Children*. Unpublished thesis. University of Illinois, Urbana, 1964.

JAHODA, M. "The Meaning of Psychological Health." *Social Casework*, 1953, *34*, 349–354.

————. *Current Concepts of Positive Mental Health*. New York: Basic Books, 1958.

LARCEN, S., SPIVACK, G., and SHURE, M. "Problem-Solving Thinking and Adjustment Among Dependent-Neglected Preadolescents." Presented at Eastern Psychological Association, Boston, 1972.

LEVINSON, M., and NEURINGER, C. "Problem-Solving Behavior in Suicidal Adolescents." *Journal of Consulting and Clinical Psychology*, 1971, *37*, 433–436.

MC CLELLAND, D. C. "Testing for Competence Rather Than for 'Intelligence'." *American Psychologist*, 1973, *28*, 1–14.

MEICHENBAUM, D. H., and GOODMAN, J. "Training Impulsive Children to Talk to Themselves: A Means of Developing Self Control." *Journal of Abnormal Psychology*, 1971, *77*, 115–126.

MERRIFIELD, P. R., GUILFORD, J. P., CHRISTENSEN, P. R., and FRICK, J. W. "The Role of Intellectual Factors in Problem-Solving." *Psychological Monographs*, 1962, *76*, (10).

MILL, E. *My Schoolbook of Picture Stories*. New York: Holt, 1967.

MINUCHIN, S., CHAMBERLAIN, P., and GRANBARD, P. "A Project to Teach Learning Skills to Disturbed, Delinquent Children." *American Journal of Orthopsychiatry*, 1967, *37*, 558–567.

MUUSS, R. E. "A Comparison of 'High Causally' and 'Low Causally' Oriented Sixth Grade Children in Respect to a Perceptual 'Intolerance for Ambiguity Test'." *Child Development*, 1960a, *31*, 521–536.

———. "Mental Health Implications of a Preventive Psychiatry Program in the Light of Research Findings." *Marriage and Family Living*, 1960b, *22*, 150–156.

OJEMANN, R. H. "Incorporating Psychological Concepts in the School Curriculum." *Journal of School Psychology*, 1967, *5*, 195–204.

PETERSHAM, M., and PETERSHAM, M. *The Circus Baby*. New York: Macmillan, 1950.

PLATT, J. "Interpersonal Problem-Solving and Heroin Addiction." Presented at Southeastern Psychological Association, New Orleans, 1973.

PLATT, J., ALTMAN, N., and ALTMAN, D. "Dimensions of Real-Life Problem-Solving Thinking in Adolescent Psychiatric Patients." Presented at Eastern Psychological Association, Washington, D.C., 1973.

PLATT, J., SCURA, W., and HANNON, J. R. "Problem-Solving Thinking of Youthful Incarcerated Heroin Addicts." *Journal of Community Psychology*, 1973.

PLATT, J., and SPIVACK, G. "Problem-Solving Thinking of Psychiatric Patients." *Journal of Consulting and Clinical Psychology*, 1972a, *39*, 148–151.

———. "Social Competence and Effective Problem-Solving Thinking in Psychiatric Patients." *Journal of Clinical Psychology,* 1972b, *28,* 3–5.

———. "Means of Solving Real-Life Problems: I. Psychiatric Patients Versus Controls, and Cross-Cultural Comparisons of Normal Females." *Journal of Community Psychology,* 1973a.

———. "Studies in Problem-Solving Thinking of Psychiatric Patients: I. Patient-Control Differences; II. Factorial Structure of Problem-Solving Thinking." *Proceedings of the 81st Annual Convention of the American Psychological Association,* 1973b, *8,* 463–464.

PLATT, J., SPIVACK, G., and BLOOM, M. *Means-Ends Problem-Solving Procedure (MEPS): Manual and Tentative Norms.* Philadelphia: Department of Mental Health Sciences, Hahnemann Medical College and Hospital, 1971.

PLATT, J., SPIVACK, G., and SWIFT, M. *Problem-Solving Therapy with Maladjusted Groups.* Research and evaluation report. Philadelphia: Department of Mental Health Sciences, Hahnemann Medical College and Hospital, 1973.

POSNER, M. I. "Memory and Thought in Human Intellectual Performance." *British Journal of Psychology,* 1965, *56,* 197–215.

RAPAPORT, D. *Organization and Pathology of Thought.* New York: Columbia, 1951.

READ, K. H. *The Nursery School.* Philadelphia: Saunders, 1955.

SHEERER, M. "Problem-Solving." *Scientific American,* 1963, *208,* 118–128.

SHURE, M. "Fairness, Generosity, and Selfishness: The Naive Psychology of Children and Young Adults." *Child Development,* 1968, *39,* 875–886.

SHURE, M., NEWMAN, S., and SILVER, S. "Problem-Solving Among Adjusted, Impulsive and Inhibited Head Start Children." Presented at Eastern Psychological Association, Washington, D.C., 1973.

SHURE, M., and SPIVACK, G. *Cognitive Problem-Solving Skills, Adjustment and Social Class.* Research and evaluation report. Philadelphia: Department of Mental Health Sciences, Hahnemann Medical College and Hospital, 1970a.

———. "Problem-Solving Capacity, Social Class and Adjustment Among Nursery School Children." Presented at Eastern Psychological Association, Atlantic City, 1970b.

———. "A Problem-Solving Intervention Program for Disadvantaged Preschool Children." Presented at Eastern Psychological Association, Boston (with L. Powell), 1972a.

————. "Means-Ends Thinking, Adjustment and Social Class Among Elementary School-Aged Children." *Journal of Consulting and Clinical Psychology*, 1972b, *38*, 348–353.

————. "A Preventive Mental Health Program for Four-Year-Old Head Start Children." Presented at Society for Research in Child Development, Philadelphia, 1973.

SHURE, M., SPIVACK, G., and GORDON, R. "Problem-Solving Thinking: A Preventive Mental Health Program for Preschool Children." *Reading World*, 1972, *11*, 259–274.

SHURE, M., SPIVACK, G., and JAEGER, M. "Problem-Solving Thinking and Adjustment Among Disadvantaged Preschool Children." *Child Development*, 1971, *42*, 1791–1803.

SIEGEL, J. M., PLATT, J., and SPIVACK, G. "Means of Solving Real-Life Problems: II. Do Professionals and Laymen See the Same Solutions as Effective in Solving Problems?" *Journal of Community Psychology*, 1973.

SIEGEL, J. M., and SPIVACK, G. *Problem-Solving Therapy: A New Program for Chronic Schizophrenic Patients*. Research and evaluation report. Philadelphia: Department of Mental Health Sciences, Hahnemann Medical College and Hospital, 1973.

SIMON, H. A., and NEWELL, A. "Human Problem-Solving: The State of the Theory in 1970." *American Psychologist*, 1971, *26*, 145–159.

SPIVACK, G. "Toward an Understanding of a Specific Type of Academic Underachievement." *Devereux Schools Forum*, 1966, *3*, 1–9.

————. *A Conception of Healthy Human Functioning*. Research and evaluation report. Philadelphia: Department of Mental Health Sciences, Hahnemann Medical College and Hospital, 1973.

SPIVACK, G., and LEVINE, M. *Self-Regulation in Acting-Out and Normal Adolescents*. Report M–4531. Washington, D.C.: National Institute of Health, 1963.

SPIVACK, G., and SPOTTS, J. *Childhood Symptomatology: Further Data Defining the Meaning of the Devereux Child Behavior (DCB) Rating Scale Factors*. Devon, Pa.: The Devereux Foundation, 1966a.

————. *Devereux Child Behavior Rating Scale Manual*. Devon, Pa.: The Devereux Foundation, 1966b.

STRAUS, M. A. "Communication, Creativity, and Problem-Solving Ability in Middle and Working-Class Families in Three Societies." *American Journal of Sociology*, 1968, *73*, 417–430.

Index